Ogwadabwah!

A Life Lived on the Spectrum

Angelica A. Brewer
& Edan Galbraith

Other Books by Angelica A. Brewer

Seventy Thousand Camels: A Motivational Survivor's Memoir

Ogwadabwah!

A Life Lived on the Spectrum

Angelica A. Brewer
& Edan Galbraith

Ogwadabwah! © Angelica A. Brewer, 2023

All rights reserved. No part of this publication or the information in it may be quoted from or reproduced in any form by means such as printing, scanning, photocopying, or otherwise without prior written permission of the copyright holder.

Effort has been made to ensure that the information in this book is accurate and complete. However, the author and the publisher do not warrant the accuracy of the information contained within the book. The author and the publisher do not hold any responsibility for errors, omissions, or contrary interpretation of the subject matter herein. This book is presented solely for motivational, informational, and entertainment purposes only.

First published by DoctorZed Publishing, 2023

DoctorZed Publishing books can be ordered through online booksellers or by contacting:
DoctorZed Publishing
10 Vista Ave
Skye, South Australia 5072
www.doctorzed.com
info@doctorzed.com

ISBN: 978-0-6457955-0-9 (pbk)
ISBN: 978-0-6458591-9-5 (ebk)

A CiP number can be found at the National Library of Australia.

No part of this publication may be reproduced, transmitted, transcribed, stored in a retrieval system, or translated into any language, in any form, by any means, without the written permission of the author and publisher. Understand that the information contained in this book is an opinion and should be used for personal entertainment purposes only. You are responsible for your own behaviour, and this book is not to be considered medical, legal, or personal advice. The information expressed within this book is not medical advice, but rather represent the author's opinions and are solely for informational and educational purposes. The author and publisher is not responsible in any manner whatsoever for any condition that may occur through following the opinions expressed herein.

rev. date 14/08/2023

DEDICATION

For my children, Alycia, Kristen, Edan, and Sabrina

FOREWORD

This story is about a mother's deep love for her autistic son. As a young child, Edan was diagnosed as being on the autism spectrum with some learning difficulties and a natural talent for imagination and drawing. Adel deeply loved her son and ensured he benefited from family and professional support. The prognosis was optimistic during his childhood years as he progressed along the autism spectrum to what used to be described as Asperger's syndrome.

Unfortunately, some autistic adolescents undergo a psychological transformation during or soon after puberty. The pre-teen is making considerable academic and social progress with only minor concerns regarding emotion regulation and management. During puberty, the brain is re-wired to attain cognitive, social, and emotional maturity, and there is a deluge of puberty hormones. However, for some autistic adolescents, during the rewiring and changing hormonal systems, something happens to the emotion regulation system. Anxiety can reach an intensity that is not effectively reduced by cognition, psychological therapies, and medication. The teenager experiences extreme distress that they, their parents, and professionals feel is out of control.

The autistic teenager has a catastrophic emotional reaction to specific experiences, such as particular sounds, being offended, perceived injustice and uncertainty. There is a release of powerful emotional energy that is quite frightening for parents and the autistic person themselves. The destructive behaviour is a means of expressing and discharging the intensity of the agitation and acts as a temporary 'reset' button.

Autistic adolescents can also experience considerable distress in seeking but not achieving social connections and feeling like they are an alien in a hostile world. A coping mechanism for social isolation is to create and escape into an alternative imaginary world over which you have control and can experience social success. They must also cope with new body sensations and sexuality without an understanding of the complex social codes associated with expressing sexuality.

Autism in adolescence can then become 'autism plus', with recognition of additional mental disorders such as an anxiety disorder, especially obsessive-compulsive disorder, depression and self-harm, and a personality disorder. The clinical profile changes, and parents feel they are losing their connection with their autistic son or daughter, who is deeply distressed and agitated. Behaviours may emerge that do not seem to respond to sedative medication or cognitive behaviour therapy, and the police and residential psychiatric services are often involved in supporting and protecting the autistic adolescent, their family, and the community.

As Edan went through traumatic autistic adolescence and experienced the darker side of autism, his mother, Adel (Angelica), was a consistent source of love and support. She had to cope with her son's extremely disturbed behaviour and the effects of that behaviour on her family. Edan and Adel are the heroes of this story, and they are also my heroes.

Professor Tony Attwood

INTRODUCTION

Dear reader,

Thank you for choosing our book. I hope you like it and that it connects with you.

Edan Galbraith is my son, the youngest of my three children and a wonderful person whom I love very much. Edan was born with a developmental disorder that affects how people process information, mostly on a social level. At the time he was diagnosed, the developmental disorder had the name 'Asperger's syndrome'.

Asperger's syndrome now sits within the Autism Spectrum Disorder continuum and has lost its diagnostic name. I personally feel Asperger's syndrome should retain its name, for in my opinion, it differs from autism in many ways. There are people walking among you every day who are Asperger's sufferers, and you will possibly never know it because the outward signs are not always distinguishable. *Aspies*, as they are affectionately called, are great mimics.

Although Asperger's syndrome has lost its diagnostic name, because Edan grew up understanding himself as having Asperger's, and because I feel there are distinctions between Aspies and other people on the autism spectrum, in this book I will use the terms Asperger's syndrome, Asperger's and Aspie.

Unlike some other Aspies, Edan's Asperger's syndrome is quite evident. He also demonstrates some more classically autistic tendencies. I spent the better part of our lives together trying to find *cures* for Edan's condition instead of accepting and enjoying his uniqueness and the richness of his character.

Having a child with Asperger's syndrome also highlighted to me how many other parents out there have children with this condition, parents who more often than not keep silent until someone comes along and says, 'My child has

Asperger's.' This book is designed to reach out to those parents, and also to people who have been diagnosed with Asperger's syndrome or Autism Spectrum Disorder.

As no two children have the same characteristics, this book will speak more to some than others, but it will nonetheless speak to the struggle of a parent, learning to live with, understand, and love their Asperger's child.

The epilogue to my journey is the recognition that we *all* have a little Asperger's in us, and that graceful acceptance is the *only* cure. If someone is going to be unfavourable, this will be the case whether they are a neurotypical or an Aspie. Asperger's sufferers are not bad or broken.

This book is divided into three parts. The first part is my story as Edan's mother, with excerpts written by Edan and a few significant others, plus lots of photos of my precious boy.

The second part is a collection of original anecdotes and stories written by Edan on a variety of topics given to him by me in order to demonstrate how an Asperger's mind might think. Some are very humorous and, in my opinion, direct and logical, yet others will definitely challenge your own definition of the subject matter. Here too, I have included various samples of his amazing art.

The third part is devoted to a number of contributors who have offered their take on Edan, having known him intimately, or having kindly shared their personal ASD journey.

Part Four is an expose in how additional diagnoses of Complex B Personality Disorder and Pathological Demand Avoidance, as well as sexual expression through fetishism, begins to wreak havoc in Edan's and our lives as an Aspie adult.

I hope you learn something about your own precious Aspie as you read this book, but more importantly, that the book calls out to your attitude toward Asperger's syndrome—or even about how you might see yourself.

ANGELICA A. BREWER

TABLE OF CONTENTS

Dedication		v
Foreword		vii
Introduction		ix
PART ONE	**Angelica's Edan**	**1**
	Birth of a Little Alien	3
PART TWO	**Edan's Edan**	**81**
	15 to 17 Years of Age	83
PART THREE	**Everyone Else's Edan & Other Journeys**	**107**
	Pat's Edan	109
	Other's Edan	127
PART FOUR	**The Darker Side**	**139**
Epilogue		181
Edan's Mentally Ill Story		191
Acknowledgements		195

PART ONE
Angelica's Edan

BIRTH OF A LITTLE ALIEN

On the 3rd of March 1996, at 07.47am, Edan Khaellan Galbraith tumbled out of my tummy into an awaiting world. He was my longest labour (48 hours), and my biggest baby—weighing in at 4.3kg.

Edan was by far my easiest pregnancy. His father and I were never an ideal couple. My previous two pregnancies, those of Edan's sisters, Alycia and Kristen, were fraught with discord, tension, and emotional unrest. Alycia's birth required every intervention known to man, short of a caesarean. Kristen was born jaundiced, and was the smallest at just 3.48kg. Both were 22-hour labours.

Edan was a nagging request by his father to have a son. He was the last male in his father's line, and so he wanted a son to continue the family lineage. I could understand his concern on some levels, but I wasn't ready for a third child.

I had been bullied all my life. First by my mother, then by the other kids when I arrived in Australia from Italy at the age of nine, then by employers, and finally by my husband. I possessed a bad temper and a strong sense of indignation that made me reactive, but I lacked the proactive personal tools to stand my ground. Eventually, I would give in to my tormentors as a way of escaping continuous persecution and manipulation.

I was thirty years old when I made the decision to have my third child. I had to be rather firm about this being my decision so that I did not resent this pregnancy in the way I had resented my second. Kristen too had been a demand by my husband. Alycia, on the other hand, was the result of poor contraception. Only two years after her birth, I was definitely not ready for a second child, given that our marital issues remained unresolved.

In order to ensure that this pregnancy resulted in a boy, we followed a recipe given to us by a close family friend. I was somewhat sceptical about this recipe, but when I read the entire book, it made real sense. We followed the method to the letter and I fell pregnant immediately. I recorded the exact conception date: May 29th 1995, at 11.01pm.

My pregnancy with Edan was all smooth sailing, and because I had yet again appeased my husband, he was very accommodating towards me over the entire gestation period, and our fighting was significantly reduced. Edan's birth too was easier, albeit longer. I did not require a single stitch or medical intervention outside of generic midwifery. Edan was actually delivered by a family friend who had five children of her own.

We knew we had a boy early in the pregnancy because the ultrasound produced at thirty-five weeks showed a definitive penis. However, holding my chubby, perfect little man in my arms was added relief. Hopefully, my husband would now let me be! When we met he joked about wanting his own football team.

Edan was a good baby who, unlike his sisters, breastfed well and ticked every box for a healthy baby.

One day, when Edan was about nine months old, I was changing his nappy when I suddenly caught his gaze. His big caramel eyes looked deeply and unflinchingly into mine. For a strange moment that seemed to last forever, I felt as if my son and I were one, somewhere inside a time continuum that hovered above our consciousness.

I then heard myself say to him, "You're not from this world are you, Edan?"

Edan's eyes did not leave mine, as if to acknowledge the obvious.

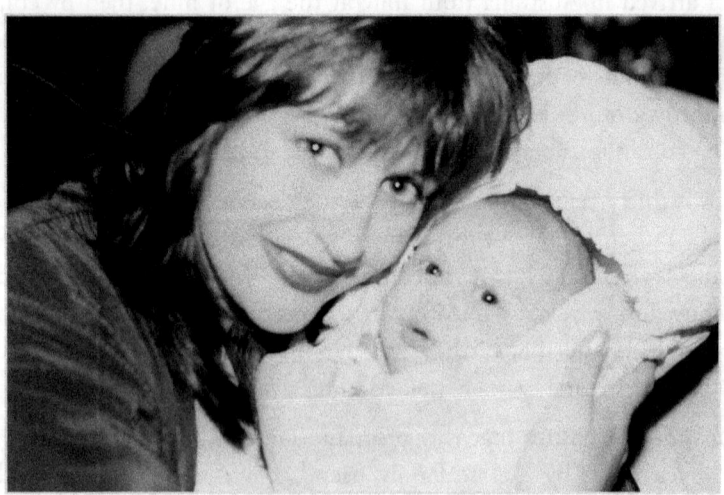

A very proud mum indeed

FRIDAY 22nd of MARCH, 1996, 11.09am

My dearest little Edan,

Hello, my angel, this is your mummy, Angelica, writing to you for the very first time. I had meant to do so throughout my pregnancy with you, and up to now (you are almost three weeks old) but I've been so busy looking after you and the rest of our little family that I just didn't get a chance to until today. I also want you to know that I am typing this letter to you rather than writing it by hand because it is quicker and less strenuous, and not because I'm being impersonal. I did the same thing at the start of your sister Kristen's diary.

Let me begin by saying that we are all so happy to have you, and that you are the most spoiled of the three children as far as visitors in hospital, presents, and follow-up phone calls go. You're the 'big boy' everyone has been waiting for, and you've certainly created a lot of excitement all around.

You were born EDAN KHAELLAN GALBRAITH on the third of March 1996 at 7.47a.m. You weighed 4.3kg and measured 53cm long. You are therefore the heaviest of the three children, although Alycia, your eldest sister, beat you by 3mm in length. All my children were overdue, but you really took the cake (and substantial portions of my patience) by being 11 DAYS OVERDUE! I went into the first stage of labour on Wednesday the 28th of February at around 1am, but I did not reach the second stage of labour until about 3am on Sunday the 3rd of March. I have to admit that even though your birth was tedious and testing, it was also the easiest, but I must wonder why you took so long before deciding to bless us with your wonderful little presence. Is it really that cosy in there?

We used a fertility recipe to conceive a boy, but if you had been a girl, the name we had picked out for you was Rhiannon Sian. This brings me to my next topic—your name.

Throughout my pregnancy your dad and I racked our brains trying to come up with a name for you. I have always loved the name Aiden, and Aaron was a second choice, but daddy didn't like Aaron, and thought you might get called Aids if we named you Aiden. Of course I don't agree with this, as I'm of the opinion that if kids are going to call you a name they'll find something. You'll probably get The Garden of Eden with your current name, even though it's spelled differently.

Daddy liked these names for you: Dillon, Brandon, Rhidian, Taylor, and Heath. I don't like any of those names, especially not Dillon or Brandon.

We searched and we searched, and for a long time settled on Liam, with Aiden as your middle name. But then Daddy got sick of Liam, so we borrowed books from the library on topics like Medieval English, Scottish, and Irish history in order to find something interesting that would suit your strong-sounding Scottish surname (Galbraith).

Right at the last minute before your birth, we settled on Edan, which was fine by me because it is the Celtic spelling for Aiden. Edan means fire. Khaellan is daddy's own spelling of another Irish name, Cailean, which means Colin in English. Auntie L, your daddy's older sister, is responsible for finding Cailean. So now you know how we came up with your name.

I certainly hope you like it.

I almost forgot to mention you were born in Auburn Hospital which, naturally, is in Auburn, where we have now lived for the past four and a half years.

Now let me introduce your family. Your daddy is thirty-two years old and was born in Campsie, New South Wales. He is employed in media communications, which is a job he enjoys—and a very exclusive one at that. My full name is Adalgisa Angelica Galbraith (nee Gemmellaro). People at school I had a lot of trouble with the pronunciation of my Christian name, so I shortened it to Adel when I was seventeen years old. I am thirty years old and I was born in Rome, Italy. I immigrated to Australia with my mother and grandmother when I was almost ten years old. At the moment, I work part-time as a sales consultant in a showroom specialising in wedding cakes. The owner is a long-term friend of the family. I first began working for him in 1984.

Your eldest sister is Alycia Felicity Galbraith. She is seven years old and was born in Paddington, New South Wales. She is very school-oriented and enjoys drawing, reading, and karate. Alycia currently holds a green belt in karate and is determined to work her way up to black someday. Your other older sister is Kristen Danielle Galbraith. She is four years old and was also born in Paddington—the hospital closest to where we lived at the time (Petersham). Kristen started in kindergarten at Alycia's school this year, St John's Catholic School in Auburn. She also enjoys drawing, reading, and playing SEGA. Kristen is currently enrolled in one of Sydney's most renowned children's modelling agencies, and although she still hasn't been signed up to any TV commercials or photo shoots, she has been in high demand for castings.

Kristen is a little temperamental and tends not to pay attention to what she is told, which is why she is not being selected for final productions. We are very proud of your beautiful and intelligent sisters, and I am certain you'll follow in their footsteps where brains and talent are concerned. You already are as handsome as a three-week old baby boy could possibly be. So far you look like your daddy, who is also handsome, although he thinks he isn't, but that's only because he has no taste.

Other parts of our family are Alycia's cat, Tommy, who is four years old and is grey and white, and Kristen's cat Sebastian, who is nearly two and is all black. My own special pet is McBird, who is a little yellow canary. He sings beautifully. Daddy doesn't really have a pet, but he likes to breed budgies. So far he has eleven of them outside in our aviary. I can't envisage whether you'll get a pet of your own, mainly because we don't have the room or the resources to accommodate another animal, but I'm sure Alycia and Kristen will let you share their cats. At the moment, you're much too little to be worried about that. Maybe we can get you a goldfish or an ant farm?

As I am half Italian and half Spanish by birth, this makes you and your sisters' one half Australian, one quarter Italian, and one quarter Spanish, an interesting mix of nationalities. Your star sign is Pisces, Alycia's is Libra, Kristen and I are Taureans, and Daddy is a Capricorn. I'm really into astrology, and when I meet someone new I just can't help myself, I have to ask them their star sign. I am also very interested in anything to do with the supernatural, although I am a Catholic and probably should not be interested. I have my views on religion and I don't always adhere to what people and books tell me. I draw my own conclusions.

Our little family is a group of individuals in their own right. We are all very different and selective, but we are all talented and opinionated. I am certain you too will stand out on your own and be whatever you aspire to be when you are an adult. All your father and I wish for you and your sisters is that you are happy, safe, healthy, and prosperous in life, and that you steer away from social evils and pressures. Unfortunately, you kids are born in an era where there is increasing violence and a breakdown of morality and values, but with enough love from the both of us, and the right amount of discipline and ethical upbringing, you three will hopefully rise above all of this human misery. Your father and I love you children more than anything in the world, more than ourselves and our own parents. We try hard every day to bring you up properly and to the best of our abilities. So if anything goes wrong later on in your lives, it will not be because we failed you as parents—at least I hope not anyway. There is nothing either of us wouldn't give up or that we would not do in order to embrace your little lives, and to protect and nurture you all. You and your sisters are blessings in our lives. Before you were all born, we were just ordinary people living ordinary lives. Now we feel special, and we thank God every day for our three wonderful, beautiful, and extra special children who must be the envy of everyone on the planet. Well, that's my opinion.

So Edan, I had better close my first entry into your diary now. Let me finish by saying that besides being the little Adonis of the southern hemisphere, you are also an extremely well-behaved and loving little baby. You sleep most of the day, waking up only to feed (I am breastfeeding you), and you don't even mind it when you have a dirty nappy.

At night you were only waking up once or twice for your feed, and this isn't taking too much of a toll on me physically, although it would be great if you could sleep right through like Alycia did as a baby. I'm sure you will sooner or later. Everyone I have spoken to scared me with stories about how naughty little boys are compared to girls, but so far I have another little angel to add to my list, and as far as I'm concerned, I am the luckiest mum in the whole wide world!

I love you so very much, my darling son. You have made me a very happy and fulfilled woman and mother. God bless you.

With endless love,

Your Mummy

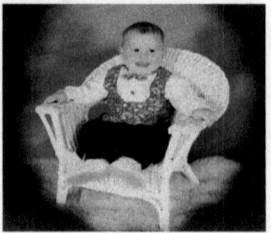

Edan's christening outfit

Diagnosis

Family life, with Edan as an added distraction, plodded along fairly steadily.

My marriage wasn't improving, but I had my beautiful children. And truly beautiful they were.

Edan had those caramel eyes I have already mentioned, and the pinkest skin. His hair was copper with a hint of blonde, and you could see tiny freckles forming. A throwback to my biological father—a man I never met.

By the age of two and a half, Edan had reached all of his milestones. I was ecstatic when he bed wetted only once after removing his nappy. Edan was a good eater and overall, a happy, adventurous boy. Edan had become the benign male presence that had been missing all of my life. I showered him with kisses daily. I was totally in love with the child I didn't think I wanted.

One day, I was watching a home video of my girls, when something struck me. Their vocabulary at Edan's age appeared much larger than Edan's.

It is a popular consensus that boys develop more slowly than girls, so I threw this off as generic fact and thought nothing more of it.

Until Edan began pre-school.

Edan attended a welcoming little prep school in St Helens Park where we lived. He started off in 'Tadpoles'. There was little, if any, separation anxiety, and I never received distress calls from the staff. Then one day the call arrived.

"We would like to hold a meeting with our director, Mrs Galbraith. There are a number of things we'd like to discuss with you regarding Edan."

I gulped. What could possibly be wrong with my quiet, unassuming little boy? Okay, I remember once before we moved from Auburn, Edan trotted towards me and with one angry sweep of his hand sent a vase flying from the coffee table, but I put that down to him mimicking his father's behaviour whenever we fought.

I tried my hardest to avoid fighting with my husband, often giving in for the sake of peace. However, there were arguments that were truly ferocious and destructive that all the children witnessed, and I thought some of this angst could have rubbed off on Edan. I prayed Edan wasn't bullying the other kids at pre-school.

The staff cautiously and gently asked me whether I had noticed certain habits at home with Edan, such as constantly lining things up and other repetitive behaviours. Yes, Edan liked to line up his foam blocks and then place his father's model cars neatly on top of the blocks, bumper to bumper. So what?

And yes, Edan would watch the same video over and over. Don't all kids have a favourite video or book?

The staff reported Edan running from one end of the room to the other in a perfectly straight line, utilising intentional timing and calculation. He did not interact much with the other children, shunning them or sometimes projecting aggression when approached. He displayed systematic interest in select activities or toys. Additionally, Edan's language skills were not 100% age appropriate. Oh, and he walked on his tippy-toes all the time!

Then out came the word:

AUTISM.

What the hell? Is that like that Dustin Hoffman film or something?

Nahhh, no way! My son is not like that! What do these people know?

Edan and his beloved foam blocks

Drum Roll!

Edan was required to go through various government-funded testing phases and places. The first being with the New South Wales Department for Education and Training, to which Edan was referred by the Early Childhood Support Service.

Edan undertook The Griffiths Mental Development Scales Test as I watched intently, hoping this was all just one big mistake and that my son was perfectly fine. Edan's behaviour was good throughout the testing. I was glad, because he had recently begun to demonstrate frustration by banging his head against walls or furniture and, a number of times, he threw things he was holding angrily and deliberately. Typical behaviour for a boy, right?

The test was divided in six subscales: Locomotor, Personal-Social, Hearing and Speech, Eye and Hand Co-ordination, Performance, and Practical Reasoning. Edan was only non-compliant a couple of times. He uttered many clear words, and on occasions he did repeat words and phrases the way he did at home. Now and again Edan ritualistically held some of the blocks he had been given to play with, pushing them together and then pulled them apart. This was his 'train doors opening and closing' habit, which fascinated him so.

I received the results by mail, dated Monday the 29th of November 1999.

These were the determinations:

Chronological age - 42 months

Overall Developmental Age - 30 months

Locomotor (Gross Motor) - 34 months. Edan jumped from the height of two steps, walked up stairs with one foot on each step and walked on tiptoes. He did not balance to stand on one foot, hop, or balance to walk along a line.

Personal-Social (Self-Help) - 32.5 months. Edan says his full name and age. He can undress himself, put away toys, and open doors. Edan does not cooperate well in play with others, use all cutleries well, or manage buttons.

Hearing and Speech - 25.5 months. Edan listens to stories and during the assessment he named common objects and pictures. Edan did not speak in sentences, explain how to use common objects, or repeat sentences.

Eye and Hand Coordination - 25.5 months. Edan built towers

with small blocks, imitated circular scribbling and threw a small ball. He did not imitate the drawing of vertical or horizontal lines, thread small beads, or cut paper with scissors.

Performance - 33 months. On this scale, Edan completed simple form board tasks in which he placed shapes in the correct spaces. Edan did not open and close a screw lid container, or build with small blocks to match models.

Practical Reasoning - 30 months. Edan identified money and repeated up to two digits. He did not count a small number of objects, or show understanding of 'bigger', 'big', 'little', 'higher', or 'longer'.

Edan's overall developmental age was found to be within the Mild Developmental Disability range, and the results on the Hearing and Speech, Eye and Hand coordination, and Practical Reasoning scales were significantly below his age level. Edan received a referral for ongoing speech pathology assistance and a recommendation for participation in a structured early intervention program.

His paediatrician, located at the Campbelltown Public Hospital, delivered a final diagnosis.

Edan was found well within the Autistic Spectrum Disorder range.

*Edan and his sisters, Alycia and Kristen
Christmas 1999*

I wasn't entirely convinced, but no less concerned. I decided to go directly to the only other people I knew would have gotten to know Edan as well as I did, namely the ones who highlighted his problem to begin with: his pre-school assistants.

I put together a questionnaire for his teacher, Katrina. This is the exact transcript of that questionnaire:

Dear Katrina,

I have compiled this questionnaire in order to help me understand Edan a little better so that I can form my own opinions, and not just listen to those made by academics and medical experts. You and the rest of the staff probably know Edan better than anyone else, bar his family, therefore your opinion is ten times more valuable to me than that of the practitioners.

This questionnaire has been compiled entirely by me. These are the questions of an anxious, doting mother, and in no way did I receive assistance or advice from anyone, neither did I plagiarise the questions from a medical text.

I desperately need to understand Edan so I can help him in and out of the home environment. I am torn apart by the autism diagnosis, which I consider the worst type of neurological disorder. I do not see many autistic traits in Edan, and on some days I feel he is not autistic at all! Simultaneously, I do not want to be someone who buries her head in the sand. Therefore, your observations will help me understand where Edan's weaker and stronger areas are. Once I accept fully what Edan's exact condition is, I can get on with the task of tackling the issue realistically and, therefore, get Edan well rather than watch him, unconvinced, and undecided, agonising over the question, 'Is he or isn't he?'

If, for ethical or personal reasons, you cannot fill out the questionnaire, I will understand. Please rest assured that this questionnaire is for my benefit only. It will not be used in conjunction with official, medical, or professional reports. Your gift of caring, empathy, and understanding is appreciated.

Yours gratefully,
Angelica Galbraith

Question 1

Does Edan understand instructions or is he merely mimicking/imitating? If he does understand, to what extent does he understand? Would you say that he tries to understand? On a scale of 0 to 10 what score would you award Edan for compliance? Is he genuinely trying to learn and join in? Does he show a real interest in what he is shown? Is he often difficult to convince? What are his favourite activities? In your opinion, what does Edan excel in? What are Edan's most significant weaknesses? Has he shown any improvement with these at all since starting pre-school?

Answer

Depending on the depth and detail of an instruction, he will understand it. For example, if Edan is asked a short, clear question or given a short, clear instruction he will follow through and/or answer you.

"Go and wash your hands'"

"What is that?" (Said while pointing at the object)

If a question/instruction like the two examples above is given, Edan will not have any problems. However, with more detailed/complex instructions or questions, Edan will show misunderstanding.

If Edan appears to not understand what is being asked of him, we will then repeat the question/instruction, making it much more detailed to specify what we are asking of him.

Edan does show an interest in learning to join in, however it is understandable that certain activities set out during the day may not interest Edan and therefore he will not want to participate, whether this be a particular craft he doesn't want to do or certain songs he doesn't like or know the words to. This is normal. If Edan does not want to participate in a particular activity, he is not made to, just the same as if it were any other child.

Edan shows a particular interest in building with blocks, and admires outdoor play a lot.

Edan's cognitive developmental area is one of his strengths. He has a great memory and is very knowledgeable in regards to colours, numbers, and prepositions (over/under/in/out). Edan's attention span is gradually getting longer, depending on the particular content of the music/language session. Edan usually gives us a minimum of five minutes' attention.

As seen in Edan's yearly (1999) report, it is evident that Edan has a weakness in his social/emotional area, which specifically reflects in his interaction skills with peers and communication with adults. This, however, could relate to having poor self-esteem, and/or a lack of self-confidence.

Edan has improved dramatically in all areas of development since he has been attending pre-school.

Question 2

How does Edan interact with other children? Is he friendly and inviting, or is he aloof, discouraging, and aggressive? Does he ever initiate play? Does he at least join in play? How long does it take him to join the children in play and does he genuinely want to? Please offer me a ratio of time spent playing with other children compared to time alone daydreaming or in solitary play. Does Edan show a preference for some children and not others? Is he affectionate with the children? How do the children respond to Edan? Do they understand him? Do they like him? Do they want to play with him or are they simply bewildered by him and therefore lose interest and walk away? What games does he like playing most, and do these games involve one or more children aside from Edan? Would you describe Edan as a happy, carefree child with an affectionate, sunny nature?

Answer

Edan does play with other children in their groups. However, he generally plays much more constructively on his own.

Edan is friendly whilst playing but tends to seek attention by peers chasing him or him chasing them. Edan tends to only become aggressive or angry with the other children when he has particular feelings and needs to express them. Edan has begun to initiate play with peers and will get them to join in—but only with selected people.

Edan does join in others' play groups freely, depending on which children, and where they are playing. These qualities will determine Edan's willingness to take part. Edan is not ever made to join in specific activities. He will do so only if he wants to. Edan spends more time playing with others than he does in solitary play.

Edan does show preference in the children that he plays with. Edan can be very affectionate to his peers and to staff also. The children respond to Edan the same way they do to any other child in the class. He is not at all singled out. The children understand him, even if not verbally. He also communicates well with gestures and facial expressions: e.g. if he wants to play with someone, Edan may grab them gently by the hand and walk with them while pointing to the particular play area that he wants to head towards.

Edan enjoys playing a lot of games outside, and some of these will be made up and have no rules at all. It depends on what game is played as to whether or not Edan plays alone or with friends. Edan appears to only play with peers in the cubby house and when he creates a game of chasings. When Edan is playing in the sandpit, he generally plays alone. The majority of the time, Edan can be described as a happy and carefree little boy who is very loving and shows a lot of affection. He has a bubbly nature.

Question 3

Does Edan throw tantrums? How often have you witnessed him hitting himself? Will he scream and become aggressive if disturbed whilst engrossed in an activity he really enjoys? Will he readily abandon an enjoyable activity to continue with something else? Does he ever ignore you as if he can't see or hear you when he doesn't want to do something? Has he ever hit another child at the centre, or thrown things around because of frustration or anger? Is he always happy to do as he is told? How well does he respond to toileting, meal times, rest times? Does he show any initiative with any of the above, especially toileting? How often does he indulge in his '*train*' ritual (bringing two shapes of the same size together and pulling them apart)? On a scale of 0 to 10 how would you rate him re: class participation, attentiveness, initiative, spontaneity, creativity? Is Edan at all disruptive? If yes, to what degree, when, and how often? Do you feel Edan has any understanding re: humour or social cues? Is he empathetic? If yes, to what degree?

Answer

Edan has thrown tantrums very rarely, this could be described as frustration. For example, when he is asked to eat something that he doesn't want/like he will clamp his mouth shut and begin to cry (that's as far as we have seen). As for hitting himself, we haven't yet observed that, however he has been seen to pinch himself excessively.

A few times Edan has been observed playing at an activity until someone else comes along to take a piece of that toy, at which point Edan screams and clenches his fist and will shake his arm and fist. Edan is free to select his own activities and, within the classroom, there are a large number of activities happening. This is in order to accommodate all the children's wants/needs and interests. What we may classify as an enjoyable activity may not interest Edan, and therefore he will move on to another activity.

Occasionally, Edan has been spoken to and/or given instructions to do something, and we will get a common response from him, as with a lot of other children, which is, he cannot hear us, or is indeed ignoring us. We repeat the request and ensure we have full eye contact with Edan. This is when we break through the 'selective hearing attitude'.

Very few times, Edan has been observed to hit, or attempt to hit, another child because of anger or frustration. This is improving as we monitor Edan and encourage Edan to use his words in order to express his feelings.

Generally, Edan is happy to do as he is requested. Edan generally responds to routines and transition times quite well; e.g. going to the toilet or having morning tea. At times, Edan will show a lot of initiative in doing what is next on the routine; e.g. go straight to morning tea before washing his hands.

A few times, Edan has been observed indulging in the train ritual and not only with shapes of the same size, he has been seen doing this a few times a day and, as a result, his eyes go cross-eyed from tracking the objects. Edan participates in class fully both in activities and group times. Even if he is not playing with groups of children the whole time he is still participating in activities. He displays initiative by selecting his own activities.

Edan is mildly attentive and somewhat spontaneous. I feel this is all due to his attention span limit. And Edan is also fairly creative with his art/craft. The work is structured, but the process of completing the final product is his own usage of creativity. At times, Edan can be a little disruptive, as too can others in the group. This occurs generally at group times when we are unable to hold Edan's attention through a story etc., but once again, this is due to his attention span limit. So naturally, once he has lost interest he will become disruptive.

Edan does have humour. He is a very happy boy who laughs a lot. He is aware of social situations and ways to behave in them. We are working on his communication skills that will enable us to assist him to resolve conflict more on his own. Edan is also empathetic to the degree that if someone is hurt/sad, Edan will want to go up to them and give cuddles.

Question 4

Is there anything Edan does that appears bizarre and not at all in accordance with normal behavioural patterns, capabilities, achievement, development, and reasoning for a regular three-year-old? Do you believe Edan is autistic? Would you lean more towards a diagnosis or condition which relates to delays in language? In other words, do you feel as I do, that Edan is developmentally delayed rather than neurologically disturbed? In what ways is Edan like a regular three-year-old boy? On the other hand, what abnormal behaviour concerns you most about Edan? Why? Do you consider Edan intelligent? Idealistic?

Answer

When Edan has a scream/fist-clenching outburst, it worries me that he does not use his words to express his needs or wants. Edan's attention span could be a little longer for his age/stage of development. Edan can reason the same as any other three-year-old. He is cognitively intelligent, as in he knows his colours, shapes, and numbers. Edan is a lot like other three year olds in his class/group in that he selects his own activities as do other children.

Edan can achieve self-help/emotional skills the same as other three year olds. In the social aspect of development, Edan is the same as his peers as he can use his manners to say please and thank you when reminded, and is able to seek help to resolve conflict. He can also share his toys with his friends. In the cognitive area of development Edan is able to do almost all the tasks on the checklist, but more importantly, he can attend music/language for five minutes, which is a big achievement.

Edan is intelligent. A good way to see this is to quiz him in the cognitive area of development, to see that he knows all of his basics.

* It is noted that Katrina would not comment on 'Do you believe Edan is autistic? Would you lean more towards a diagnosis or condition which relates to delays in language? In other words, do you feel as I do, that Edan is developmentally delayed rather than neurologically disturbed?'

Obviously, these questions were too loaded.

Question 5

Do you feel Edan should remain at the pre-school up until kindergarten age? That he is, in fact, keeping up with his peers and benefitting from the centre despite his shortcomings? Is it your personal feeling that Edan be placed within an education program that devotes more one on one attention to him, and therefore may aid in strengthening his weaknesses more efficiently? If Edan continues in mainstream school, where do you see him ten years from now? Do you believe he'll cope and go on to lead a normal, productive life?

Answer

Edan is coping well at the pre-school and has made some great improvements since attending. He has activities to stimulate his mind and body, and the social interaction with other peers of the same age/stage of development. Edan is keeping up with his peers, bearing in mind that all children develop faster/slower than others.

Edan is definitely benefiting from the centre, and this is seen by his progress chart.

* * * * *

Edan graduated from Frogs class (this followed Tadpoles) in 2001. He attended an early intervention program funded by the Sydney City Mission. Due to his attention span deficit, Edan had a hearing test, which resulted in a normal reading with very mild hearing loss in one ear due to excessive wax. His walking on tippy toes created concerns with the development of his calf muscles, and he received an assessment at the paediatric sector of Campbelltown Hospital, where he obtained his autism diagnosis. His calf muscles were still okay, but we had to encourage correct walking at home through various exercises. Edan spent a significant amount of time with an amiable speech therapist at The South Western Speech, Language & Learning Centre in Campbelltown. It was an experience we both enjoyed. In 2002, Edan began kindergarten at the St Helens Park Primary School. His first school report read as follows:

"Edan is an enthusiastic learner who has made significant improvements in his social and academic development. He has settled into the learning environment, becoming increasingly more focused, which has aided his overall progress. Edan is beginning to seek clarification when unsure of a task. He continues to require extra teacher support to verbally explain written activities and classroom tasks. Edan has made pleasing progress, and he should be proud of his efforts."

I submerged myself in hours of literature about autism spectrum disorder, even contacting a brain injury specialist in Victoria who found significant success with the reversal of severe neuro-developmentally challenged patients, via extensive and specialised body exercise configurations that realign the brain into normal working function. I found parents of children with ASD in the classifieds and wrote to them to compare their children to mine. I left no stone unturned.

But I *still* wasn't convinced Edan suffered from autism spectrum disorder.

Frogs Class Graduation Day
Candlebark Pre-School, St. Helens Park NSW

Moving Forward

In 2002, Edan's father and I separated. It was a turbulent, uncertain time, fraught with emotion and complex circumstances, but we got through it.

I did not believe Edan's father recognised that Edan may have a disability, but he also did not try to disprove the diagnosis in the way I did, and this was one of many reasons I left him.

I often tried to find an origin for Asperger's syndrome. Was it genetic? It is generally believed—but not yet proven—that autism spectrum disorder is indeed genetic, with information carried by the father and then passed onto their boys, primarily. Historically, males make up the largest proportion of ASD sufferers. Looking back, I definitely saw traits of ASD in my husband.

There was also the old tale my mother-in-law would tell me about not being able to carry boys because her blood was not compatible with her husband's blood. As a result, she miscarried two male babies. Kristen was tested a day after her birth for a similar reason, and my smallest baby was also very jaundiced. Then there were the immunisation conspiracy theories that were much supported by the left wing greenies in our community.

I soon learnt to stop leaning on the reason why, and focus more on the actual management of ASD.

Edan appeared to do well in primary school. His early intervention program and diagnosis afforded him funding for a teacher's aide and, with this help, Edan managed with a few re-occurring issues. One thing that was also repetitive in his school reports was high praise for his beautiful disposition.

Year 2 Report

Edan is an enthusiastic student. He enjoys the opportunity to share stories and is developing the confidence to ask for help. Edan is a willing participant in all learning activities. However, he requires adult direction and support to complete most tasks accurately. He has difficulty listening to directions and is still developing skills in the areas of comprehension, grammar, and punctuation. He displays difficulty in numeracy, and he will need continued support in all areas of schooling next year. Edan has worked hard to learn his sounds this year, and this is becoming evident through his spelling ability. Socially, Edan relates well to his peers in our class, but often makes the wrong decisions in the playground when influenced by other children. He has made progress in all Key Learning Areas by trying hard to focus. He should be proud of what he has achieved this year.

Year 3 Report

Edan is a happy and polite student. Edan has found most learning experiences difficult this year and will require intense ongoing support next year. He responds well to one-on-one assistance, but must remember to ask for help if he does not understand a direction or instruction. Edan is a confident speller who enjoys spelling games and activities. His oral reading is developing and his fluency is improving. Edan needs further development in his comprehension skills and relies heavily on adult support in this area. Edan finds it difficult to listen to and follow instructions and needs extra guidance to begin activities. His confidence in this area is improving, however, and he is now willing to share his ideas with the class. Edan finds mathematical tasks challenging and will require intensive support in this area next year. He finds difficulty in using concrete materials and remembering strategies and concepts from previous experiences. Edan enjoys Creative and Practical Arts, especially Visual Arts. He has produced some amazing artworks this year. It has been a pleasure sharing this year with Edan, and I wish him all the best next year.

Year 4 Report

Edan has been a delightful, happy student who has striven to achieve his personal best in all areas. He has developed definite likes and dislikes within the curriculum as he gets older, but with patience and assistance, he is able to participate in all areas, although often not at the same academic level as his peers. I have thoroughly enjoyed Edan's company this year, and I wish him success and happiness at his new school.

Edan demonstrated a marked talent for drawing, much like I did at school. His love of words also reflected my propensities, as did his dislike for maths. In school, I found myself always in trouble for not listening because of a neglected childhood, and I tended to be misled by my peers—but I did a lot of the misleading as well.

In light of everything so far, I still wasn't convinced Edan had Autism Spectrum Disorder.

The many lovable faces of Edan

Edan's memories of school and life, written on the 25th of January, 2014, aged 17.

I remember the time when I was very young how I used to go to pre-school and special disability school also speech therapy. At pre-school, I had two really good friends, one called Bronwyn and the other Max. Bronwyn and I have been really close friends for a long time because we would always come over to each other's houses and have fun together and the same thing with Max. Sadly, after a while, they both moved to different schools and that was it for us but I at least got pictures of them both for memories.

I had some really good friends at that special school too, but I stopped going there eventually so I didn't even get time to fully know them, but it's not that big of a deal. Speech therapy was quite alright and it wasn't too stressful. I then went to St Helen's Primary School and my best friend over there was Ritchie. Ritchie was a funny and nice guy to hang out with, and the hilarious thing about Ritchie was that he acts way too silly, but we had some good laughs together and lots of sleepovers at each other's houses. Ritchie was one of my best friends there could possibly be, and I still miss him.

I had a lot of really nice teachers as well, at my primary school over at St Helens Park. My favourite one was Mrs N, sadly what happened to her though is that she died, and I did not know how. I had scripture every Wednesday at my primary school and I quite liked it and understood it very well.

At home I played a lot with Alycia and Kristen, and I was happy all the time. I also really liked Tommy and Sebastian; I patted them a lot and spent most of my days playing with them inside and outside, they were very nice cats but of course they both died as well, which is very sad to see.

I liked going to lots of places with Mum and the family, and I really enjoyed playing with those foam blocks in the toy room at Gunn Place. I really loved the toys I used to play with when I was little, like the Laa-Laa Teletubby toy I always carry around, and Elmo from Sesame Street, and lots of others. I really enjoyed spending time with Mum and Dad, and showing them a lot of the funny stuff I do when I was also very young.

Eventually, my mum and dad were just not getting along anymore and ended up divorcing, and then when the time came, we moved to live in Adelaide. Adelaide is a really nice, quiet place and I loved it a lot when I was living there. We lived in a nice relaxing suburb called Springton. Springton is a place full of really good, generous people.

I finished doing primary school at Springton and then I went onto doing high school in this other nice town called Birdwood. Birdwood High School helped me a lot more than any other high school could because of the way people teach there. At my high school I work with a special teacher called Pat. Pat is an extremely nice lady who is also not just some ordinary teacher, but is also a really good friend, and most other school students in the world don't get that kind of luck with their teachers like I do. All the common teachers are always boring and don't even have long supportive conversations with you, they just only give out work to you and that's it, they don't even help you with your work that much when it's too hard for you. But with Pat, she makes my life so much easier and calm, because Pat even asks me questions like, "*Are you okay?*", and, "*Do you need to have some quiet time for a minute until you feel a bit more comfortable again?"* for when I'm feeling freaked out about being so close to everyone.

I used to have this terrible fear about people coming close to me because I keep on thinking that they were going to touch me on the face. I really hated getting touched on the face when I was young. Now I don't mind if people touch my face because Pat really helped me a lot on how to overcome my fear near strangers, and I really appreciate Pat for doing that. If I never moved to Adelaide in the first place I would never have got those special gifts from Pat and also all that support from her too, so it was a good idea for me to come and live in Adelaide.

I made a new very special friend, as well. He was also Pat's student. His name is Yanek Rachwal. Yanek's disability is problems he has with his lungs. Yanek has to take postural drainage sometimes, which is how it made him and I become best friends. To be totally honest though, he's a lot better than Ritchie, and I do mean that.

I've always remembered the times where me and Yanek went bowling and did mini golf at Tanunda. We helped each other cook in home economics at school, playing P.E. together at school and all kinds of other fun things we do together in life. Those memories will never fade and go away.

What I also like doing in life is working at Jim's Local General Store in Springton. Jim and Chris are such nice, gentle people and all thanks to Pat. She got me to do work experience in Jim and Chris' store in the first place, which is very kind and helpful for a teacher like Pat to do for me, which is what no other teacher would do for me to help me with my skills more.

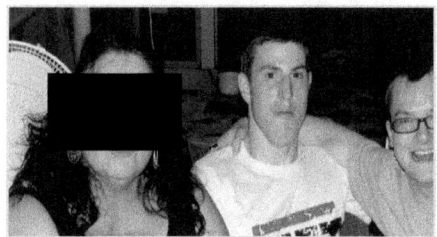 

(Left) Pat, Edan, and Yanek
(Right) A picture drawn by Edan of his two favourite teachers,
Pat and Ayden

*(Left) Edan and Yanek in class surveying a work task
(Right) Edan with a finished product from Home Economics, a
favourite subject studied at Birdwood High*

Difficult Times

The single mother life was not easy. I went from part-time work and the full care of my children to full-time shift work, a mortgage, and a nagging feeling of romantic emptiness that was obsessively filled by online dating.

There were a number of relationships that were toxic and only served to take me away from the people who really mattered; my children. I couldn't help myself, however. I was lost and needed aid, and I thought these men would give me that. Even though my marriage was a disaster, It had given me a strange sense of stability that I now found completely missing.

It was during this long, dark period of my life that my daughters helped out with Edan's upbringing. It is to them that I now throw the pen, in order to give you a panoramic snapshot of Edan's life from the age of six until I finally regrouped in 2008, moving away from Sydney and relocating to Adelaide.

In 2008, Edan was twelve years old.

Alycia Galbraith On Edan

My brother Edan is a lovable soul, and he amazes me. I become so impressed with his train of thought! Moments like these I treasure, as well as simply having him around for peaceful company.

I love my brother very much and am proud of him for his personal achievements in life. I honestly wouldn't have him any other way, as then he wouldn't be the Edan I know and love. He brings a smile to my face when he can see I really need it, and a big belly laugh at the times where I feel like letting my hair down and being silly. I wish him well in his adventures and hope he knows that his eldest sister will always be there for him! He is a good boy who lives a simple life. He knows right from wrong and is purely a bundle of innocence.

Due to his nature, when he has done the wrong thing, you can't help but smile—because it has usually been done in the sneakiest and also cheekiest way, which means it is just so humorous that you cannot get too mad at him for having done it! People often gravitate towards Edan because he is so gentle and well-mannered (most of the time!), and he truly appreciates the small treasures he is given, whether it is a new gadget or something as simple as a packet of biscuits.

Edan loves the smaller things in life and gets much pleasure experiencing them in his little world, and most of all, in his own time. I love spoiling my brother for these reasons. I enjoy watching his expressions and emotions when he receives a gift—it brings warmth to my heart! If only more people were like him! There are times admittedly that Edan's Asperger's can become frustrating, often making him hard to deal with, especially on a full-time basis, as his ticks get the better of him sometimes. However, at the end of the day, he always means well, and you learn to accept the entire package that is Edan.

I do miss the carefree and affectionate little boy that was Edan and the fun times we used to share, but people (including myself) grow and change each day, so I have come to accept the natural progression in his life and have stored our memories fondly in my heart. It sometimes makes me sad when looking back at photos and old videos, but I think about the positives that I now enjoy which weren't possible before, like deeper conversation.

Sometimes Edan comes out with things that really surprise!

(Left) Always finding it difficult to display or accept affection, Edan did his best with Alycia on his 16th birthday. (Right) A rarity indeed seeing Edan smiling in such close proximity to another human being (with sister Alycia)

Kristen Galbraith On Edan

Where to start with Edan? I guess with my earliest memories.

While I don't remember Edan's birth (and while I'm not sure I was even there), I distinctly remember hearing the news of his arrival, and becoming overwhelmed with excitement. Unknowingly, the birth of Edan would push me into the rank of the middle child, although the only thought I had at the time was the introduction of a younger sibling and brother, a new present for me, kind of like my own real life doll to play with whenever I wanted.

The first few years are hard to remember. I guess I found Edan to be a novelty at first, but it soon became clear that he was less of a playmate for me and more of a responsibility for my mum. Though I was granted playtime with Edan now and then, I had the realisation, as any young child does, that a baby has very limited vocabulary and motor skills, and therefore he became less of an interest to me.

As Edan got older, he developed many characteristics that annoyed me, such as the fact he liked to play most of the time in solitude. Many times when he was left to his own devices playing with blocks, or cars, or drawing, when I attempted to join in, he would immediately scream or throw a tantrum in distress. Sometimes, when he was forced to interact with us, he would protest by screaming, like when my dad put him in the pool and he would cling to the side, and if my sister or I tried to grab him and play, he would go berserk. I quickly learnt not to bother him while he was in this phase, which led to me being less interactive with Edan while he was in his early developmental stages.

Edan struggled to give me his full attention and even eye contact a lot of the time, which made me less interested in spending time with him. Instead, I would spend most of my recreational time playing with my sister and our friends.

My friendship with Edan improved when he was old enough to string sentences together. I enjoyed reading to Edan and participating in his creative, imaginary stories. He liked to make up words with unique movements and gestures that I had never seen anyone do before. He would also create games that had no real instructions, rules, or explanations, and as an older sister, I felt as if I were somewhat of a teacher to him, and therefore went along with them.

Over the years as he grew up, there were times where the three of us siblings would all interact well with each other as a group, but we also had individual relationships with each other too. Edan and Alycia had their own special bond, as did I with only Alycia and only Edan.

With Edan, I felt like I could tell him anything, and he wouldn't judge or make fun of me. He has always been my confidant, and to this day he can surprise me with his logical and simple advice. I have told him things I can't even tell my best friend or parents, and I have always been very appreciative of him for this trustworthiness.

When Edan started primary school and was interacting more with strangers, I felt a sense of guardianship over him that I did not have before, when my only concern about him was if he were able to play with me when I wanted. Although he already had two loving parents watching over his best interests, I felt protective of him and the people that my parents might not be aware of who could cause him harm or discomfort.

By the time Edan was four or five, I had noticed and had also had it explained to me that his intellectual condition was different. While I didn't exactly understand it at such a young age, I had been aware of his differences and had noticed that he was not like everyone else. Often, at recess and during lunch breaks when he was in kindergarten and I was about to graduate to high school, I would visit his classroom or find him wherever he was playing, and make sure he wasn't being hassled and was having fun with friends. It became one of my main priorities to check on Edan at school, and this was a priority that continued for most of my life with him.

Edan had very peculiar habits, which I found interesting at first and then annoying later. He would make up his own words and sometimes the only way to talk to him would be through talking *his* way. He would create strings of nonsensical gibberish and would have to repeat them several times before he was ready to communicate. I found this frustrating at times, and while as I got older I learnt to tolerate them more, often I would snap and tell him off for being 'weird'.

While most of the time I was calm and patient with Edan, as a child I admit I would take advantage of his handicap sometimes. To me, Edan did not have a sense of self-worth or have much emotion besides anger or happiness, and if you told him to do something he would either say 'yes' or 'no', depending on the incentive you offered. He was easily coaxed into doing something if you explained it in a way that sounded beneficial to him. And while I was also persuaded he had no understanding of sympathy or compassion, he would try to comfort me if he could see I was clearly upset by offering food or suggesting we watch a movie together.

There was a point in time when I thought Edan and I had come to a crossroad and he had reached his intellectual limits and could no longer learn anything new. He became more of a last resort of boredom to me at this time. When he reached puberty, I spent less time interacting with him in conversation and more time doing antisocial activities with him such as watching TV and eating. I guess I was at a rebellious stage and didn't have much time for siblings and I was not extremely social myself. I grew more frustrated with Edan and his habits at this time than I ever had before, though I was still protective of his feelings. I could tell he wanted to be alone most of the time too, and didn't bother trying to reconnect with him. I had my own friends and high school to concentrate on anyway.

When we moved to Adelaide with my mum, I grew closer to Edan again. I didn't know anyone in Adelaide so I spent most of my time with Edan. I believe this is when our bond grew closer and was at its strongest. We agreed on what the plans were for the day instead of me forcing my ideas onto him, and he seemed to actually want to spend time with me, unlike when he was younger. This was short-lived, however, as I moved back to Sydney only a few months after.

Initially, I was extremely distraught about leaving Edan, mainly because I thought he would have no one to accompany him in games or on walks. Although I have always been aware that Edan prefers his own company and doesn't really need or care about having friends or companions, I still worried about his loneliness. Edan had had close friends before that I could tell he enjoyed sharing time with. Under all his layers of reluctant and assertive behaviour, it was clear to see that Edan understood happiness and friendship, and what's more, it was essential for him to be surrounded by it.

I have never seen Edan more happy or content than when I've watched him around his friends. Even if they were more intellectually advanced and capable than him, it didn't matter to him as long as they wanted to play with him and accepted him for who he is. I thank Yanek for being Edan's best friend and for showing my brother the joy I never thought he was capable of feeling, and something I thought for a long time I was the only one who could bring out of him.

When I was younger, I had a realisation that maybe I had acted towards Edan as more of a mother figure than a sister. I was constantly concerned for his wellbeing and state of mind, and whether he was heading along the right path in life in order for him to succeed.

While I have limited control to determine what can be done with his future, whatever happens I trust him to be able to speak up about what he wants, and if there is something he doesn't like, he will change it—or at least indicate his feelings to someone who can help. I used to have my doubts about the way in which Edan's condition was handled, but I know now that my mother has excelled in all expectations and efforts to make sure Edan has received no less than the finest of treatments and education to assist him.

I grow prouder of my brother's intellectual advancement and improvements every day, and while I sometimes worry about his unforeseen future, I know he is in good hands. Edan has grown out from his unresponsive and isolated behaviour, and I am glad to say that he is my closest friend. I hope to one day see him have a successful career in whatever area he enjoys, be that hospitality or art. However, even if he doesn't, I will always be proud of my only and youngest brother.

(Left) Kristen and Edan in school uniform
(Right) On the Yorke Peninsula circa late 2008,
Kristen, Edan, and a very proud mum, Angelica]

✳ ✳ ✳ ✳ ✳

Angelica On Edan

The fragmented memories I held of Edan during those dark years were of a generally well-behaved boy who was super cute and lovable, even if he was frustrating a lot of the time. He was a boy who tried his hardest at school, and who gave his very best each and every day, even though he lagged behind academically. He was a boy everyone loved, even if they often teased and provoked him—myself included. He was a very solitary boy who didn't appear to need friends, but who enjoyed it when someone paid him attention.

Our home had a lot of people coming and going during that time, including Alycia's and Kristen's school friends, as well as my various love interests and acquaintances. Everyone had something to say to and about Edan. Edan just continued as best as possible. His Megasketcher became his best friend. Hundreds of pictures were etched onto it. We possibly went through four Megasketchers, until I decided he was chronologically too old for one, and forced him to use paper and pencil.

By this time, I accepted that Edan had a disability, although I did not agree on the autism diagnosis. I had Edan rediagnosed, and the new paediatrician offered an alternate label, that of Asperger's syndrome. *This* I could live with.

I was under the distinct impression people suffering from Autism were far more unreachable and less interactive on any level than those who had Asperger's. Although both conditions are social dysfunctions, I felt blessed that Edan was more of an Asperger's patient with, granted, some autistic mannerisms. Edan had various physical tics—hand flapping, finger clicking, and rigid body contortions—that placed him on the autism spectrum, but his interpersonal, emotional, cognitive, and academic propensities all belonged to Asperger's syndrome.

Often, my family and I would reprimand Edan until he'd drop the latest tic or twitch, only to discover he had begun adopting a new one that would replace it. It became obvious that this was Edan's way of comforting and reassuring himself, and also something he did whenever he was deep in concentration with a beloved activity. Sometimes it was even as a reward to himself for completing something.

At around the age of six or seven, Edan had a routine that we affectionately called 'semmen'. Edan developed a fascination with the number seven, and carried a little plastic number seven around with him everywhere. The routine involved four separate movements performed in sequence, all the while calling out the word 'semmen', which of course meant 'seven'. It was so repetitive and unusual, but we all eventually became so accustomed to it, to the extent that we performed the routine with him and even on our own. I do believe there's a little bit of Asperger's in all of us.

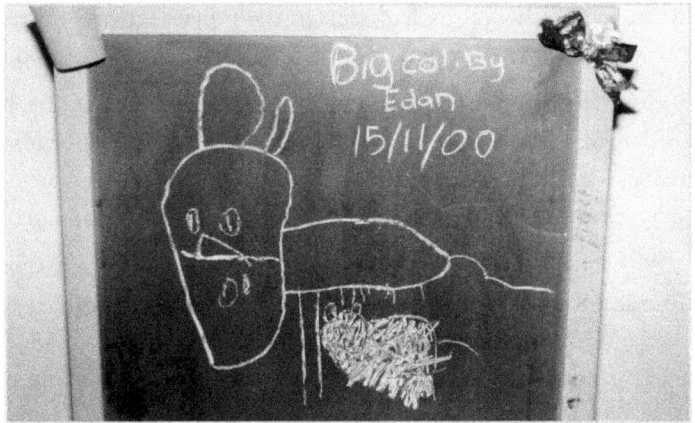

Edan's artistic bent started quite basic like all regular children

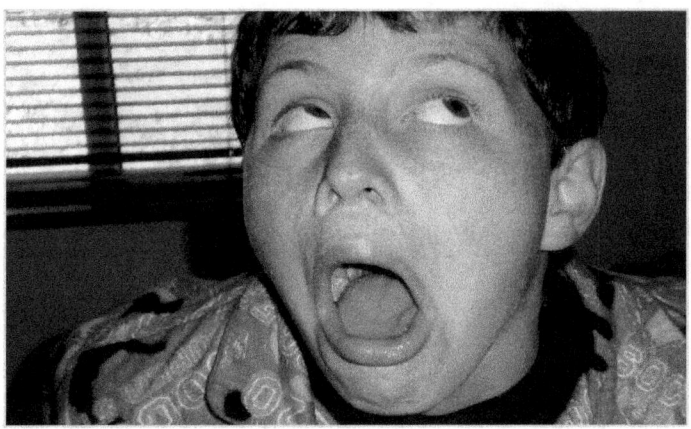

This was Edan's 'fish face', a facial tic he hung onto for a long time, and one I'm glad he has lost

What began to really shine through, however, was Edan's natural ability with drawing. He also appeared to possess a photographic memory. He would draw a lot of what he saw, pretty much to scale, without a picture of the item in front of him.

Edan was fascinated by specific things at different times. One of these was the Parisian cathedral Notre Dame Du Paris, which he first saw in the animated Disney film, *The Hunchback of Notre Dame*.

I remember being in the kitchen cooking, and Edan showing me his Megasketcher. Almost to scale, using some general details which could not be confused, was the cathedral he had seen in the movie; but the movie was not playing. It was the same with the Eiffel Tower and Sydney's Centrepoint Tower.

My girls would ask Edan to draw me or my partner at the time, and he'd record details that were poignant and characteristic, albeit sometimes embarrassing, like Nick's excessive body hair in the picture on page 34. People with Asperger's are very literal, so if you're looking for a sugar-coated response from them, you're *not* going to get it!

I made some terrible mistakes with Edan. I refused to believe he could not see beneath intended humour. All the books kept harping on about Aspies not understanding humour or abstract topics, and that one had to be linear and literal for Aspies to fully grasp what you were telling them. And yet everyone agrees that Aspies have normal intelligence, so how did the two gel? I didn't understand, and I'd be damned if I wouldn't try doing things *my* way and bust that myth!

So one afternoon I rang Edan from work and using a worried, urgent tone of voice, I told him there was an intruder in the house, and to take the cordless phone and hide outside until the police arrived. Edan said 'yes' and that was it.

I was working in Murray Bridge at the time, and the trip home was approximately 45 minutes long. Around twenty minutes after I made the prank call, I rang home to tell Edan I was only playing him, expecting him to get the joke. But, there was no answer from Edan. I then realised my mistake and continued calling until I arrived home. There was still no answer.

I looked all over the house, upstairs, in the outhouses, along the streets. No sign of Edan. Then panic set in as it was getting dark. I jumped inside my car and drove to the next town. My partner (now my husband) did the same.

Then it dawned on me.

Edan would sometimes go to his old Primary School in Springton and sit on the swings to think and be alone. If he were *truly* afraid, he hopefully had hidden here.

Lurking in the shadows as I called out his name repetitively was my son. Edan looked at me furtively and pulled out the home phone from his pocket.

"It didn't ring," he told me innocently.

No, of course it wouldn't, my darling boy. It was out of range. It's not a landline phone. Guilt swallowed me up, and I hugged him even though he struggled with that. I apologised for the rest of the night, reassuring Edan that this would never happen again.

"I really thought there was a murderer in the house, Mum, and I thought that if I went far away enough he would not find me. I thought if the police came, they wouldn't need me there anyway, so I hid."

Big heavy tears fell from my eyes onto his rigid shoulders. What a crappy mother I was. I tried to explain what pranking was but he didn't understand the concept. And why should he? Why should I try and justify my ridiculous actions?

"You mean you were joking, Mum? That is not a joke though. A joke is something written down in a funny story or something. You know, something that makes you laugh."

I had tricked my son once before when he was much younger.

He had worms and was absolutely terrified of them. Medication had only helped slightly, and they continued to reoccur for some time.

Whenever he misbehaved, I used his fear as a threat in order to make him compliant. It worked every time, but it also amplified his paranoid feelings to a point where he became certain he had worms inside of him *all* the time.

My daughters jumped on board with this in order to control him. We all called this punishment, 'Sending Edan to the worm factory where buckets of worms would be poured onto him'.

We had another control method called 'Going to gaol'. It was none other than time out for him, but it involved Edan lying across the dining chairs on one side of the table. The chairs would be pushed into the table, locking Edan in. Edan had to remain there until he was told to come out. It was one of my daughter's ideas. It was they, after all, who had to put up with Edan's obsessive/compulsive manias and occasional tantrums while I was at work. Because Edan took everything so literally, when the girls would then add the scolding, "And you can stay there forever!" Edan would do just that. He'd accept his fate quietly without moving. There were times the girls forgot about him and Edan spent far too long in that predicament. This was undisputed, albeit unintentional, child abuse, and I am ashamed of it.

(Left) Edan then branched off into cartooning
(Right) And got better...

(Left) And better...
(Right) And better...

I was in a miserable position internally and though I did try, I was not giving out good mothering. I relied too much on my middle child for Edan, only because Kristen's innate disposition never argued against it. I was too preoccupied with chasing romantic love and getting bills paid to even notice what was actually going on.

Life was one huge whirlpool and my beautiful son was caught in it, and yet he kept on going. His school report cards were continued testament to his unadulterated sweetness and innocence. Edan went to bed when he was told. He put away his toys. He was still happy and loved his family in his nonverbal, nontactile kind of way. His greeting cards to me were full of beautiful words. Edan was the most loving son anyone could ask for, and I did not fully appreciate it. My greatest preoccupation with Edan, still, was to make him *normal!*

BIRTH OF A LITTLE ALIEN 35

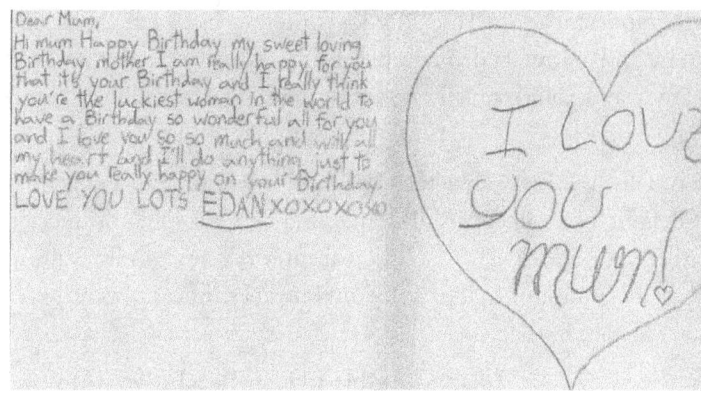

Love!

Storms Clearing

Edan was forced to adjust to a string of my failed relationships.

He did well, considering Aspies despise change. I do not believe change was truly one of Edan's problems. He'd had so much of it already in his life so far.

After his father, with whom Edan maintained a loving relationship with regular contact, there was an awful attachment to an online beau I met, named Nick.

Nick was the type of relationship a woman, married way too long and desperately unhappy for longer, jumps into. A fly-by-night gratuitous encounter over a chat room, which sounded too good to be true. It was. But like everything that happens in life, it served its purpose at the time, and Nick was good to Edan and the girls.

Nick was affiliated with an outlaw bikie gang. He was also a drug addict, although none of this was even remotely evident in the beginning. Nine months later the relationship ended, in big dramatic tears and total exhaustion.

Then Enis came along. He was the complete opposite to Nick. Clean living, tidy, perfect in every way.

Edan wasn't so keen on him because Enis, being rather obsessive himself, could not tolerate Edan's repetitive habits, tics, and poor hygiene.

Four months into our relationship, Enis admitted there was no future for us because he was not coping with Edan. I refused to accept this, and selfishly promised to begin work on my son! Of course I didn't do this, because my son was more important to me than any love interest, but I felt that I needed Enis desperately, and I stretched our relationship to two years by accommodating Enis in any way I could, mostly by seeing him when my children were at their father's.

Eventually, the inevitable occurred, and it was time to say goodbye to my Turkish delight, as I called him. For me, it ended horribly. I found it harder to cope with than Nick's exit. With the exception of my family, Enis and I had everything in common, and I was convinced I'd find nobody like him ever again.

After we had split, I had a terrible night when I gave in to the deepest, blackest emotional pain. I called Enis at work. It was a shocking phone call. I took it so badly I began to hyperventilate and couldn't breathe. When I got off the phone, I called Kristen, who was not at home. She was so frightened by my hysterical gasps that she hung up and called Edan on his phone, commanding him to run into my bedroom and administer CPR to me.

The poor little mite looked so concerned. He started blowing into my mouth as hard as he could, but more spittle came out than breath. I'm sure he had no idea what he was doing and was only copying something he might have seen on TV, but he did his very best. Again I felt the deepest shame.

"Maybe we should call an ambulance!" he called out to Kristen, while still on the phone to her.

Edan is nothing less than an earth angel. My earth angel. We didn't call the paramedics, everything calmed down, and we went to bed.

Next on the romance scene was Jeremy, a colleague from work.

By this time, I had given up on online dating. It was like playing Russian roulette. You don't know when you're going to get a decent win.

Jeremy had a disabled child himself. His daughter was wheelchair-bound, and severely restricted due to premature birth and cerebral palsy. Our relationship was doomed from the beginning. Jeremy genuinely loved me and wanted us to succeed, but I was fighting my own anxiety problems, as well as struggling to meet his daughter's needs, manage my son's disability, care for my daughters—who were now beginning to show some of their own emotional cracks—alongside running a home, maintaining a job and mortgage, and coping with Jeremy's serious but well-guarded bipolar disorder, which sometimes spilled over into our work. Jeremy was, after all, my supervisor in a girl's juvenile justice detention centre.

Being an outdoors enthusiast, naturalist, and professional hiker, Jeremy projected some of the hopes he held for his only child onto Edan, who although mentally handicapped, was fit and able-bodied.

The very first thing Jeremy suggested and helped facilitate was for Edan to join the Scouts. Of course, I held my doubts about this, but it turned out that the semi-regimented routines and Scouting expectations were exactly what Edan required. He responded to them beautifully. Edan's Scout leaders were wonderful people who truly went that extra mile to ensure that Edan was left out of nothing, and that the other boys treated him, if not with affection, then with marked respect.

Jeremy also appeared delighted to take Edan on hikes, camping, and to do general "man stuff" with him. Because of Jeremy, Edan was finally introduced to dogs, a relationship he thoroughly enjoyed. Our household only ever had cats. Jeremy's dogs, Matilda—a Staffy—and Bob—a Labrador—became Edan's best friends and a reason for getting out of the house on his own.

One time, Edan was picked up by a schoolteacher who recognised him walking along the very dangerous Appin Road where we lived in St Helens Park. He was at least six kilometres from home, heading north towards Appin. Holding onto Bob tightly in the car, Edan explained to the teacher that he was heading to his scout hall to show Bob where he was having so much fun on Tuesday nights.

Jeremy and I went from bad to worse very quickly. Sick of broken relationships, however, I clung onto him, until we decided to try something different in order to make things work; living together.

I sold my house, which was a relief, and moved myself, Edan, and Kristen into Jeremy's house, which was in the same suburb. Alycia had already moved out, soon after she had turned eighteen, following a bitter feud between the two of us.

We lasted two months. Jeremy's daughter, although living with her mother, was an awful teenager to deal with when she was around. Sometimes she and Edan got on well and other times she picked on him, calling him weird and other things. *Now there was the pot calling the kettle black!* I thought. Jeremy allowed his daughter to misbehave, and his bipolar symptoms were more pronounced than ever. In just eight weeks we had fought more frequently and harshly than in the eighteen years I was with my ex-husband.

The straw that broke the camel's back was when Jeremy began to traumatise Edan and Kristen with his obsessive cleanliness, and their inability to utilise his home comfortably. I decided my kids had seen enough of these spectacles already. I found a house to rent in nearby St Helens Park.

That last year in New South Wales became a very difficult one to deal with. The job I loved was a complete war zone because of Jeremy's lurking shadow and, as a result, I appeared on the managerial radar far too often. Not a good thing when one is trying to further one's career. Jeremy refused to let me go, and was persistent in trying to rekindle our romance. Fifty per cent of the time I would fall back in, but one hundred per cent of that time I regretted it.

My life was an utter nightmare. I had to get out. Of *EVERYTHING!*

In a matter of precisely five weeks, I bought a home in Springton, in the lower Barossa Valley of South Australia, I threw in my job, read Jeremy the riot act, and abandoned everything I had known and loved in Sydney.

Edan was enrolled to complete the rest of Year 4 at the local Springton Primary School, which was a tiny rural faculty. I had no idea what Kristen would do in terms of schooling. She admitted that she had wagged such a huge part of Year 12 and was going to fail the course anyway.

Hopefully, a brand new life in Adelaide would reveal all for all of us.

*One of the many activities that Edan became involved
with at Scouts, circa 2008*

Before leaving Sydney, I thought I had the job I had applied for waiting for me in Adelaide. Just before we left, I found out that I had failed the first part of the testing. The truck was booked, the mortgage papers were signed and paid for: I had no choice but to forge ahead.

I didn't know it then, but this was one of the best decisions I had ever made for both me and for Edan.

A visit to Thredbo with the Appin Scouts

Acceptance

By this stage, I understood that my son had a disability. I did accept it, but I never lost hope that something might magically change in him, or that a cure might be found someday.

Edan had a new teacher, who poured a lot of his energy into him. We called him 'Mr B'. Edan had been blessed with great scholastic support throughout his young life. Alas, as he grew older, Edan's disability became more pronounced—especially at home.

School was getting to be less fun and more work. His Year Six school report card from Springton Primary School read as follows:

Edan finds difficulty working in a class situation. He is unable to work next to others at a desk, which limits his peer support. He is easily distracted, and he is often not willing to attempt tasks unless closely supervised.

When focussed, he is able to produce extensive written work. Grammar and spelling is very exact for his age. He appears to have a photographic memory for words and for images that have clear New Brunswick (NB) cartoons. He responds to one-on-one learning situations completing tasks to a satisfactory standard. He has taken to following students who he likes in the yard, making physical contact on his terms.

He is now willing to engage in extensive informal conversations and ask questions of peers, when at a safe distance from others. He appears to be happier in class.

But his Year Seven report sounded a little more hopeful:

Edan is becoming more socially aware. He is gaining organisational skills that help him to stay on task. He is beginning to recognise social cues more frequently and is able to articulate his interpretation of events. Edan is starting to explore areas outside his established art skills. Edan is beginning to explore computer programmes which require peer assistance and interaction. He is gaining greater understanding and acceptance of social norms.

Kristen recognised Adelaide, especially the area we lived in, was not for her, and returned to live with her father in Sydney a few months after her arrival. In the meantime, Alycia recognised life with her father was not for her, and made the big trip over from Sydney. Edan thus lost his best friend and gained a nemesis.

Edan and Alycia's relationship was different to his and Kristen's. Whereas Kristen was more of a buddy to him, Alycia was more of a matriarch, and so as Edan's budding puberty made itself known in spite of his disability, so did his defiance.

While Edan was finishing Year Seven, I applied for and was accepted into the South Australian Department for Correctional Services, graduating as a Correctional Officer in September 2009. It was one of the proudest days of my life. I truly believed I was fulfilling a very important role that assisted in keeping the community safe.

In December 2009, in spite of the strong personal resolution never to date another colleague, I met and fell in love with a fellow officer, Adam Brewer, ten years my junior and three years in the job.

I had completely given up on men before this, and was reasonably happy being single. As with Edan's disability, I finally accepted that life without a romantic relationship would be okay.

Adam was the real deal, and even though I pulled everything out of the bag to alienate him and sabotage my quickly growing relationship with this man, he did not budge and soon moved into our home. Edan appeared fine with this, and Adam reciprocated in turn. Not ever being exposed to Asperger's syndrome, Adam was somewhat perplexed by Edan's myriad of mannerisms and his complete aloofness, but being with me was a package, and Adam was more than willing to help where he could.

Scouts Certificate of Appreciation

Edan resumed Scouts, joining a group at a suburb in the Barossa Valley called Nuriootpa. I could feel early on that he wasn't going to receive the same intense one-on-one he had enjoyed at the Appin Scout group, so it wasn't long before Edan began branching off on his own during unsupervised group sessions. The other children didn't attempt to include him when this happened.

At school, there was also a group of kids who had started to make life difficult for Edan. Edan never spoke about it, but I picked up on it, because it was much harder getting Edan out of bed for school now than when he had been in Mr. B's class. I was also copping some outbursts.

"I don't want to go to stupid dumb school anyway!"

It was around this time that I noticed Edan's hygiene becoming worse. He smelled of urine almost daily. I asked a doctor to check his penis in case he had developed a serious urinary tract infection, but everything appeared fine. In retrospect, it's possible that Edan was making himself smelly in order to be left alone. I saw this happen with some of the prisoners I dealt with at work.

One thing I learned about Asperger's syndrome involved the subject mimicking perceived social norms (from various sources, namely television) in order to appear to fit in. This mimicking often comes across as mechanical and peculiar to an audience. I believe this imitating is what created Edan's persecution at school. In essence, it's outright bullying, something Edan evaded in NSW, but life in tiny, rural towns has its disadvantages. The children knew that Edan and another boy, Owen, had disabilities. They just didn't understand how it affected them—nor did they try to find out.

I was about to let them know.

I caught the offending group in the act when, hearing strange noises coming from the balcony upstairs, I went to investigate. The group was goading Edan to jump off the balcony, and I could see that Edan was struggling to resist. In his sweet little head it was probably important to do this in order to be welcomed into the group. I called out to Edan and ordered him inside. I then told the group that if ever I saw them messing about the front of my house again, there would be serious trouble.

Had Edan given into their cruel intentions he would have surely broken something in his skinny little body.

As Edan's concerns grew, I eventually pried more information out of him. The ringleader was a boy called Jason, and it was this boy Edan feared most. I spoke to the school principal, who was absolutely disgusted with the news, and she proceeded to warn both Jason and his parents that bullying was a criminal offence in South Australia. The bullying ceased.

The damage was done, however. Edan's personality and hygiene steadily worsened.

Yet, in the midst of this crisis, Adam and I went from strength to strength in our relationship. There was nothing this man would not do for me. I was totally in love with him. I've never felt so at peace. It seemed sad that now that I was stable, Edan was growing very unstable.

Edan graduated from primary school and was enrolled into the only high school in the district—Birdwood. Edan had to catch the bus into school. I was gripped by anxiety for him. If primary school here was proving a little toxic for him, then how was he going to fare amidst the social politics that is and has always been high school? I had adopted the role of class clown to cope in my secondary years. What role could Edan adopt?

In South Australia, Edan's disability did not afford him any funding, and therefore he did not receive a teacher's aide. I registered Edan with Autism SA, and they sent a psychologist to the school for a complete assessment. Edan was found to be on the high functioning end of the autism spectrum, which completely denied him any real funding. He received a mere two hours of assistance once a fortnight. I was beginning to see why New South Wales referred to South Australia as a backwater state.

One day, Edan came out with some news. I asked him how high school was for him and he replied, "It would be okay if Jason fucked off!"

I was shocked. Edan never swore. A few times when he was little he had said to me, "What would you do if I said the F word, Mum?" To which I would reply, "I'd give you a smack!"

So one day he came over to me, extended his hand and said, "Give me a smack, Mum." Confused, I gave his hand a firm tap. "FUCK!" Edan screamed at the top of his voice. Realising Edan's rationale, we all rolled around in laughter. Bad parenting again on my part, I know, but you just had to see the humour in this.

So Jason was at it again, and he had two cronies working with him as well. Cowards!

I decided to do the good citizen thing and reported my concerns to the principal, explaining that this behaviour had continued on from primary school. It appeared that nothing was done about it, because the persecution continued. I'd had enough. How dare these heartless bullies hurt my son!

Jason lived in our township, and I knew who he was. Returning from work with Adam one afternoon, we saw Jason walking up the main street with a friend. Adam is six foot five inches tall and weighs 145 kilos. Both of us were in our correctional officer's uniform, which made us look pretty much like cops.

We pulled up next to Jason and got out of the car, heading straight toward him. Adam puffed out his massive chest and we gave Jason a piece of our mind right there in front of his friend. The kid, short of pooing his pants, appeared pretty damn scared.

Edan never experienced trouble with Jason or anyone else at the school again. In Year Nine we found out Jason had actually become Edan's mentor and token big brother. Amazing what a uniform and some good old-fashioned discipline can do!

Edan really enjoyed life in Springton after that. He loved solitary walks around the quiet little town, where waking up to birds chirping each morning was a regular occurrence, along with the distant bleating of sheep and mooing of cows.

Whenever school holidays arrived and it was time to visit his dad and Kristen in Sydney, Edan often complained about leaving. He just wanted to stay in his little township and enjoy nature.

Edan's life was one-dimensional. Basically, it consisted of school, homework (which was something he struggled with), jumping on the trampoline, and video games. I took Edan out of the Nuriootpa Scouts two years on, when I realised it was not helping him create social networks. I also decided Edan needed a little job to build self-esteem and add a second dimension to his simple, lonely life. I designed a flier and posted it around Springton and nearby Mount Pleasant.

It wasn't long before a lovely lady named Jenny called our house.

Jenny and her husband Daryl owned a property off the beaten track out the back of Springton. They had a young son. Jenny was a primary school teacher who had experience with ASD children. The couple had an entire host of odd jobs to do around the property that Edan could help with. I was ecstatic.

The city of Adelaide is like one big country town. Everyone seems to bump into everyone else somewhere along the way. So when Daryl came to pick Edan up one day, Adam recognised his face immediately. He had played football against him several times in the past.

Working for Jenny and Daryl enabled Edan to learn a few things about life on the land, and he was paid handsomely for his efforts. Adam and I saw a new Edan emerge for a while.

Daryl and Jenny enjoyed having Edan around and gave us excellent feedback about him. The strange thing was that everyone who met Edan thought he was an absolute angel with impeccable manners and a willingness to do anything that was asked of him. This was not the case at home.

Adam and I noticed Edan's progressive laziness and rudeness towards us, and set up a list of chores for him to complete around the house. The chores were not unreasonable, and we were willing to compensate him with a monetary reward. Although oblivious to the unit value of money per se, Edan knew that the gold ones would buy him something substantial at the corner shop.

Edan's first love by his own admission is *FOOD!*

Around the age of twelve it became obvious that Edan had developed what can only be described as a cheese phobia, or 'turophobia', as it is medically termed. It all started with pizza—something Edan used to love when we visited the 'all you can eat' Pizza Hut outlets in Sydney.

However, on one occasion, we noticed Edan turning white as a sheet at the sight of the stretchy cheese, then swaying as if about to faint. It was hard to understand this sudden reaction, and we discounted it as a ploy to attract attention. It also didn't make sense that Edan would eat certain cheeses and not others. It wasn't until Edan *did* faint during Home Economics class at Birdwood High that we took his condition seriously.

Edan had fainted and hit his face on the corner of the kitchen bench, creating a nosebleed. The school registered turophobia as a medical alert on his file following the episode. My family and I stopped teasing him about cheese and went out of our way to avoid further incidents. Unfortunately, Edan fainted once more at his friend Yanek's house, putting a hole in the wall of their newly built home.

Edan explained to us that white stretchy cheese, basically cooked mozzarella, reminded him of shark's tripe and therefore turned his stomach. According to Edan, other types and colours of cheese were okay. He particularly liked Feta Cheese, but the Australian variety, not the creamy Danish Feta. Strange. The aversion later included Big Mac cheese as it was too yellow, and so Edan's beloved McDonald's meals, the same ones he drew as a small boy, had to be ordered sans cheese until a few years later on when Edan got over it all again, and the Big Mac cheese could be re-introduced.

Researching Asperger's and phobias, I discovered that the cheese business was all about dealing with certain textures. Obviously, this shark's tripe was very offensive to Edan's sensibilities, much like having his face touched.

One question that remained unanswered, however, was *where had Edan seen shark's tripe?*

Edan's favourite foods depended quite heavily on refined carbohydrates, such as pasta, bread, biscuits, and cereals. He loved pretty much anything junky and sugary, and yet his favourite luncheon consisted of a large leafy salad with feta and tuna.

Little by little, Edan's menu became more exclusive, to the point where I asked him to write down what *not* to make for him. In typical Edan fashion, the result was random to say the least:

Osso buco (spelled Awsobooko)

Pasta bake (even though it has pasta in it)

Chicken schnitzel

Mashed potato (again this reminded Edan of the dreaded shark's tripe)

Corned beef

I once read a mini autobiography in Edan's school journal:

"Food is my most favourite thing in the world."

Funny that. Edan was so skinny, he was almost skeletal. Where did all that food go?

Edan struggled in the big classroom at Birdwood High, and on parent/teacher nights, we received similar reports to the ones we had got from Edan's other schools. Edan was co-operative and polite, but easily distracted, and he struggled to understand. One teacher who must have been missing in action when debriefed about Edan's Asperger's even said:

"I have done everything I can for Edan. It is very frustrating, but I can't reach him!"

Hmmmmmm. Helloooo? Asperger's? There is no one who can *truly* reach Edan.

Homework was a particularly difficult task for Edan, who had made home his sanctuary from the demands of the outside world, where more often than not, he'd wear a socially accepted 'mask' in order to cope. To continue with the demands of school once he was back in the comfort of home was quickly sending him round the bend.

* * * * *

Adam and I noticed a phenomenon about Edan's morning routine. Not only was it difficult for him to get himself out of bed, it would take almost an entire hour to just get dressed, let alone to have breakfast and get his teeth brushed. We rarely got a decent sleep. We slept in afternoon shifts because of the succession of noisy rituals Edan had to complete before moving onto the next task. To a stranger, Edan may have looked like an absolute lunatic. He would continue in this way right until the point where our driveway met the bitumen. The second he stepped over that line, Edan became transformed. His clapping and body contortions ceased, his face gathered composure, and not a peep was heard from him as he made his way to the bus stop. Just like that, Edan was a 'normal' boy. The same happened in reverse when he came home—he was a 'normal' schoolboy until he stepped over that magical line.

I found it almost impossible to help Edan with homework, so my wonderful Adam began to intervene. Adam was a saint and spent many hours trying to simplify homework instructions for Edan.

Mathematics, my old nemesis as a school kid, was also Edan's worst subject. On more than one occasion, despite Adam's indelible patience, Edan cracked under the pressure and self-harmed by hitting his head repeatedly with his fist. It was painful to watch, and I wasn't going to let my son go through further anxiety over work he might never use in life. Adam and I spoke to the school, and in term two of Year Nine, Edan was placed in Special Ed with another young man called Yanek Rachwal, under the supervision of two teachers, one of whom was a teaching assistant named Pat.

The Final Report For Year Nine, 2011

Edan has worked on a modified individual program this semester. He has achieved a number of goals such as cooking, drawing pictures with a purpose, and working with Mrs G in Art. He has also been instrumental in the management of the school flag, ensuring it is raised each morning and collecting it in the afternoon to put it away safely. He is working on his social skills and, at times, is able to initiate a conversation with a peer. The DVD which highlights his achievement is attached. Edan will continue to operate on a modified program as a Year Ten student in 2012. Edan has been quite vocal in home group. Always punctual, well-dressed and polite, his organisation has improved, and he is a willing participant in class activities.

At last, Edan's Asperger's was accepted by all!

(Left) A local advertisement looking for an after-school / weekend job for Edan (Right) Edan proudly shows his running race ribbon award at the school sports carnival alongside his equally proud, newfound friend Yanek Rachwal

Edan and Yanek in the school's agricultural program—a much welcome break from the classroom

My beautiful son was smiling again, and for a while some normality returned to our home as I continued to celebrate the success of my sixth romantic relationship, which was about to enter its third year.

Edan's tics and self-stimulatory habits were still there. He loved his trampoline and would jump on it, almost trance-like, for hours, singing long tunes that had no melodies. I often fretted about the monotonous disturbance he was causing our neighbours, but to my surprise, I did not receive a single complaint. One neighbour actually commented on how pleasant she was finding his 'beautiful singing'.

Edan would happily return home from school. You knew he was home because the moment he stepped over the magic line, his loud clapping and noises would begin. Edan's latest nonsensical exclamation as I'd open the door to him was something sounding like 'OGWADABWAH!' He'd clasp his hands together and look at me cross-eyed as he said this at the top of his voice. It really sounded like an affirmation of happiness. However embarrassed I may have felt regarding our neighbours, hearing 'OGWADABWAH' made my heart sing! My son appeared more settled than he'd ever been. All was good in my life. If only Kristen would return to live with us, or at least nearby.

Asperger's was now no longer a death sentence in my mind. I loved Edan so very much and could not imagine a son who was not exactly like Edan. I realised more and more that the problem of Asperger's syndrome lay within me and not him. I was the one who fretted about his loneliness, his disassociation, and his singular special interests. Edan loved and rejoiced inside his little world.

Edan's honour duty

There's A Problem With Adam

My all-time personal dream came true. During a visit to Sydney, Adam asked me to marry him. Alas, this happy occasion was tarnished by a tragedy. Only four days later, we found Adam's father, Alan, dead in his flat. He had suffered a massive heart attack.

Alan's sudden passing wasn't the only occurrence that took the edge off this joyous occasion. Edan's behaviour deteriorated almost immediately we made the announcement.

Adam had a theory about this. He believed he had passed my 'use by' date on a relationship, and instead of leaving like all the others, he was actually staying forever! Edan would no longer be the man of the house.

Edan began placing his fingers in his ears when we spoke to him—especially when it came to Adam's directives. If we would combat this behaviour by raising our voices to be heard, Edan would drown us out by screaming out words such as, "What? What? Mum, Mum, Mummmm what did you say, Mum? Muuuuummmmm!"

Unable to communicate with Edan amidst the cacophony, I would walk away, but Edan would then follow me around the house almost maniacally, continuing to scream at me. This rather intimidating behaviour was aimed exclusively at me, and never directed at Adam.

Eventually, Edan stopped talking to Adam altogether, let alone answering any of his questions or taking instructions from him. My beautiful life was falling apart once more.

Edan's hygiene was now worse than ever. He was dribbling in his pants and the smell of urine became unbearable. Deodorant was unheard of, and showers were a game involving Edan lying on the bathroom floor listening to the water running instead of washing himself. His feet, already deformed from years of tippy toe walking—albeit with the intervention of orthotic therapy—were dirty and fungal. His beautiful curly auburn hair had to be reduced to a number three-grade haircut because he simply wasn't shampooing it. His hands were always sweaty and greasy from clenching and clapping them nonstop, and his knuckles were red raw from the constant clasping. Edan would go through the motions of brushing his teeth, but the plaque build-up was the worst our dentist had seen in a long time.

If Adam and I did not run a bath for Edan, and place a change of clothes in the bathroom for him, Edan would put the soiled jocks and socks he had just taken off back on. Preparing a bath was our only hope of getting some of the dirt and stench off him, as he soaked in there for up to an hour. This also saved us a lot of money in water bills. Edan then got into the habit of locking himself in the bathroom or toilet in order to be left in peace. Eventually, we had to remove the locks to get him out.

Bedtime became another nightmare. It was a process of up to two hours, first with getting Edan out of the bathroom, then with actually getting him into his bedroom and into bed with the lights out. Edan would sneak his iPad into his room and play games until the early hours of the morning, so that when his alarm went off for school, he either ignored it or slept through it. With both Adam and I doing shift work, it was an additional toll on our reserves to wake up early to ensure Edan did not miss the bus. The strange thing was that when we weren't home, Edan always seemed to get to school. This was defiance absolute!

For a while after his voice broke, Edan had adopted a fake monotone to disguise his real voice. We grew used to it. Now, however, his voice was so deep and gruff it was often difficult to understand what he said—if he said anything at all.

Adam had gone through Edan's iPad once to monitor what Edan was accessing. What he discovered was hours of footage in which Edan had recorded himself playing his favourite video game on the 42-inch television. In this footage, Edan was the third person commenting on the action. It was the first time I heard his normal speaking voice. Edan also used an exaggerated American accent.

At the prison, I had met a colleague's son who spoke with an American accent. He mirrored many of Edan's mannerisms. I remember his parents worrying about what might be wrong with their young boy. I knew, but I did not dare utter the 'A' word. They'd find out soon enough, as I did. It was uncanny just how many parents I knew in that job alone who had children with ASD. I had attempted to organise an ASD prison support group, but was met with obvious resistance. Like me, these parents had to come to terms with their children's disability in their own time.

Was Autism Spectrum Disorder a sudden epidemic? Or was it always there, lurking in the shadows, since the medieval times of the village idiot? As a practicing spiritualist, I also came to know these children as the 'Rainbow Children', which was the term used by Doreen Virtue, a spiritual doctor of psychology. According to Doreen, they were the new generation of highly sensitive young people.

Edan stopped watching videos, because he claimed he could not stand our background chatter or the noise of the television programs we watched in the room adjacent to his. He now spent all of his free time on his iPad with earphones on, playing the same games over and over, drowning us out. Edan's complete isolation was his only activity. At times, I could not locate Edan inside the house and I'd find him curled up in our tool shed outside, deeply engaged in trance-like imaginary activities, which reminded me of scenes from spectral films I had seen. It was, to say the least, very uncomfortable for me.

Edan refused to eat with us and had to be fed separately. He claimed our chewing and swallowing noises were excruciating to listen to. He later developed another habit, in which he would not drink with his meals because the sound of the fluid going down his oesophagus made eating his food impossible. As a result, the urine that stained his pants and jocks was more concentrated in odour and colour because he was not getting enough fluids. Edan was also found to be urinating over his balcony at night, instead of going to the nearby toilet. This was discovered when we hired a window cleaner and the poor man was trying to scrub streaks of crystallised urine from the windows below Edan's balcony.

Possibly the worst trait Edan developed towards me personally, and one that posed a genuine concern for my safety and peace of mind, was when I'd play tag with him (a game his father had created called 'Got You Last') and he would 'tag' me by touching or grabbing me inappropriately on the privates or breasts. This sent shockwaves through my body. I felt extremely violated and concerned about the direction Edan might be heading in. I notified his father immediately, but Edan didn't stop.

Edan said some disturbing things like, 'I want to touch your privates' and, 'I'm going to put my hands all over your body'. I'd yell at him and attempt to brush it off as more of his other nonsensical rubbish, but deep down I was quite alarmed. Edan had long had an obsession with 'black hands', and strange talk about black hands coming out of the water or going under the car. It seemed that now the black hands were to be placed on me. This was not on. I wasn't putting up with that.

I realised Edan was sixteen and going through puberty, and that sexual thoughts would be visiting him, but that these thoughts might be vented on me was unacceptable. I often asked Edan if he was interested in girls or would want to marry and have children someday. Each and every time, I always received a firm *'NO!'* His iPad also revealed no more than a once-off search for 'sexy girls' on Google.

Fortunately, these incidents were few and far between and eventually stopped altogether. I put them down to Edan being in a misguided phase, and just part of his many adjustments to life and growing up.

Below is an apology note I found on the kitchen bench from Edan following a fairly brutal verbal spat that occurred between us:

Mum, I'm sorry about what I said to you before. It will never happen again. You really would believe someone like me would say someone's coming to rape you. I was being inappropriate and I'll make it up to you, I swear. I love you very much in a very grown up way, not the little kid way, and I'm sorry again.

Love

Edan

Were these inappropriate outbursts perhaps payback for the times I scared him with the 'worm factory' and the 'murderer in the house' prank?

[A drawing by Edan showing the black hands coming out of the water (or in this case a bathtub)]

I did find a few pornographic cartoons in his schoolbooks, which he had drawn of male classmates, but they were so eccentric they made no sense at all. *The bi-product of an Aspie imagination*, I thought. Edan was spoken sternly to about these drawings and nothing similar surfaced after that.

Adam, who had previously got on very well with Edan, was now at a loss as to how he should handle him. It was obvious it was Adam that Edan was targeting.

After some strong words between the two favourite men in my life, I came down the stairs to review the situation and was met with Edan's steely eyes.

"I don't like Adam anymore, Mum. I want you to break up with him."

This certainly posed a major dilemma for me. After years of romantic failures and personal pain, I had found a man who was so good to me that I still pinched myself every morning to prove to myself Adam was not a dream. But now, one of my children—the one who needed me most and who had lived with me his entire life—this child rejected the love of my life completely, and for no real reason. The only recourse I could think of was to threaten Edan that I would send him to live with his father in Sydney if he didn't start behaving. I was certain this would work, given how much he loved Springton, our big house, his school, his friend Yanek, and his part-time job.

It was a major mistake on my part.

An Encounter To Remember

From Adam

February 2014

At the time of writing this, I have known Edan for just over four years. In this time, I have seen a lot of changes. Some good, some not so good, and some that cannot be explained! Beneath all of Edan's behaviours though, lies a good-hearted boy struggling to come to terms with the world in which he lives, but at the same time coping in his own way with Asperger's syndrome and the onset of manhood.

I met Edan after I met Angelica, who I worked with at the time. Angelica and I had been on a few dates, and I had started spending more time with her, and consequently, Edan. I will be the first to admit that Edan's behaviours were frustrating, to say the least. Due to his condition and obsessive-compulsive attributes, his 'quirks' were ever-changing and hard to keep up with at times.

We seem to notice a rough pattern of changing behaviours, which appear to surface every three months or so. From washing his hands almost constantly, to flicking switches on and off repeatedly, to opening and closing doors ten times or more before finally closing them, this was a boy who did things his own way at all times, (well, nearly) and at his own pace.

Edan has always been most comfortable doing solitary activities such as playing electronic games, going for walks, using his iPad, and drawing. He is a fantastic artist, by the way, working either from memory or by copying. He is so solitary. Edan would state how he actually looked forward to school holidays when both Mum and I had to work during the day so he had full rein of the house.

Many times, we have caught Edan doing things that are interesting to say the least, but he denies these, as if embarrassed by them. One that pops into memory is his recordings of himself on his iPad while playing games on the PlayStation. I reckon he picked this up off YouTube. He would commentate the game in another accent while recording it. He would then watch it over and over again, but whenever someone else came into the room, he would pause it immediately, again as if ashamed.

One night, both Angelica and I thought that someone else was in the house, the voice was that convincing! Apparently it's not uncommon for Aspies to adopt another voice. Edan has chosen a voice similar to Mr Bean's, I think, and I can count on one hand how many times I think I have heard his natural voice.

Probably the biggest 'issue'" with Edan is his hygiene—or lack thereof. We are constantly reminding him about this, and I'm sure he gets as frustrated with us as we do with him. Showers were—and sometimes still are—an impossibility, because one of his habits is to walk into the bathroom, turn the shower on and basically stare at it while still fully clothed.

Many times I have lost my cool with Edan over this matter, and it continues still. We have found that a bath seems to be the answer, but even then, getting Edan to actually wash is nigh on impossible, and we sometimes have to be content with a soak only. I am convinced that Edan hates us nagging, but until he does something about it we will have to continue in order to get things done.

I have had some long talks with Edan in regards to many things, and although he claims to understand, I often wonder if he does. Sometimes I think it's just laziness on his part and sometimes it's his condition. It just depends on the scenario, I think.

About a year and a half ago, Angelica and I went to an all-day seminar presented by Tony Attwood, an Asperger's syndrome expert, and the very first thing we learnt was that we can't do anything about Edan's Asperger's. I know our hearts sank a little when we heard this, but Tony helped us understand the psyche of an Aspie and ways in which we can deal with it, rather than Edan.

One other positive thing that came out of this valuable seminar was a drug called Risperidone.

Risperidone is a drug intended for treating schizophrenia in low doses, and is also used in managing autism and the associated symptoms of anxiety and irritability. In Edan's case, it was recommended to help control what now appeared to look like Tourette's—his 'tics' and contortions, which seemed to intensify in the evenings, prior to routines like meal times, bath, and bed time.

Risperidone assisted Edan with settling him down at night, and I believe it also allowed him to cope better with his obvious issues, which were distracting him from leading a semi-normal life.

Finally, some peace for us as well as for Edan.

Between the Risperidone and Tony Attwood, we were given coping mechanisms to better deal with Edan's Asperger's and raging teenage hormones.

Edan is not so different from any boy his age. He has the same thoughts and feelings, but he just finds it harder to express these verbally. This is why Angelica and I have turned to the written word in order to help convey ideas, thoughts, and feelings to Edan via letters or emails, to which—much to his credit—he responds in a fairly eloquent manner.

However, his conversation skills have also improved in the past twelve months, and this may be due to the fact that Edan has been living back in Sydney with his dad. Whatever the reason, we believe it's a good thing, as things got very hairy prior to his relocation. We have noticed that on his last sojourn to Adelaide, Edan slipped back into some of his old habits. I think this is because he has found his comfort zone once more with Angelica and me, and this reignites his lazy side. His sister Kristen, who lives with Edan and their father, reports that Edan is rather afraid of his dad, and therefore he does not engage in as intense habits there as he does with us.

Edan is currently not taking Risperidone, which could also be a significant factor for the degree of recession.

Whatever happens in the future, Edan will always be Edan, and we will always love him.

His loving Stepdad,

Adam

Adelaide Oval climb a few years on from when Adam was considered 'the enemy'

Exasperated by Edan's behaviour, I asked him whether he was upset by the fact that Adam and I were getting married, and that he was now going to be a permanent fixture in our lives. Knowing Edan wasn't going to say much verbally, I asked him to write how he felt down.

The following letter seemed to address the both of us rather than isolating a specific problem with Adam per se.

I wasn't convinced.

Edan

"You're always getting in my way when I'm trying to enjoy and have fun with things, and you never give me a break. You're always getting me to do all the hard work while you're probably having nice cold drinks. And I definitely believe in the future that you'll get me up out of bed in the middle of the night and get me to do hard work for you. It really ruins my day, and I rather yous leave me alone for about a year and I really hate hearing raised voices everywhere I go around the house. It's just only that I really don't like yous telling me off every second of the day and that yous should make life a lot more fun and not so difficult.

You'd rather work a lot more than having fun which doesn't bother me, I'd rather you like working a lot more than having fun, but when you always make me do it for you. I don't feel bad at all; just stop always doing this at least. Picking up pears, and doing the electricity sheet. Don't you think that's a bit too much? I'm sorry. This is how I feel, that's all. THE END!!"

I then asked Adam to write directly to *Edan*:

Letter 31/07/2012

Edan,

It seems you don't want to talk to me but I have to tell you some things, and I need you to reply either on your iPad or the computer.

Firstly, I am not trying to be your dad. You already have a dad, and I do not want to take that away. I just want to be a friend who helps Mum to care and look after you.

Secondly, about the time I grabbed you; I did this because I honestly thought you were going to hurt Mum, and that is something that will never happen when I am around. I'm sorry if I hurt you in any way, but I was only protecting Mum! Please know that I will stop any person from hurting anyone in our family.

Lastly, I know you hate me yelling at you, but I can't help it if you have your ears covered. It would be much easier if you listened to us and then did as you were told. Then we wouldn't have to shout or yell. Good behaviour gets rewards and bad/rude behaviour gets nothing and has consequences. It's that easy. I want us to get along.

Your mate,

Adam

The 'grabbing' incident involved me finding some pictures of Edan when he was a small boy and exclaiming how cute he was when he was 'that little'. Edan lunged at the photo album, ripping it out of my hand. Adam's reaction was instinctive, and Edan believed he was trying to assault him. Adam never laid a hand on Edan that day, bar restraining him. This seemed to be a defining moment in Adam and Edan's relationship, and it was from this moment that Edan insisted he wanted to leave Adelaide and return to Sydney to go and live with his father.

Edan began to vehemently deny that he was ever a young person let alone a human being. He referred to himself as 'Air', and he could not tolerate any other form of personalisation.

On the first of August 2012, the day after reading Adam's letter, Edan replied on the computer.

Edan

Adam,

I feel a lot more better that you said you're trying not to be my father because I thought you really were trying to be, since I now know that you're marrying my mum, but the reason why is because if I stayed living with Mum, I would have to live with you all the time and a lot more than my dad, and when Mum, me, and you go out to places, I don't really want the other people walking around thinking that you're my real dad because it's just you who's walking with me and my mum. Also because I want them to think you're my stepdad and that I'm not related to you and I look nothing like you, which is true, but apart from that, that's good you're not taking over.

I trust you that you only grabbed me because you really thought that I was going to hurt Mum even when I wasn't going to, but I was only just trying to quickly snatch that photo album of me off mum's hands because I don't like her seeing pictures of me as a small kid and Mum embarrasses me about it.

I can't help blocking my ears from you and mum because I just can't stand the noises and sorry if we won't get along sooner but hopefully we will get along in a while later. I'm sort of more used to the noises at Dad's than here because there's less birds in cities and the TV that's on at my dad's isn't always that loud as you and mum usually have it.

Despite this exchange of apologies and explanations, Edan's behaviours did not improve.

There was another altercation between Adam and Edan, involving Edan not getting out of the bathroom for literally hours. Adam, tired and frustrated, forced his way inside and physically removed Edan who yelled at him.

"Get out of my life you big fat bald man! You're far away from me! I wish you never existed! You don't exist! I don't see you!"

This outburst upset Adam greatly, and in the following week I began to entertain life without Edan with some inner relief. Edan was collecting new and bizarre behaviours by the day. He could not tolerate hearing anyone cough, sneeze, or sniff, and would go crazy when any of this occurred. Once he even grabbed me really hard across the face while I was driving, forcing me to pull over in order to avoid an accident.

There were certain words he decided he did not tolerate such as, *sick, sad, love,* and some others. If I then said, 'I'm sick of your behaviour Edan,' he would chase me around the house screaming out. 'Mum, Mum, did you say sick? Say you didn't say sick! Say it!' This situation would gain momentum if I didn't concede that I said sick and then repeat the sentence utilising a replacement word.

A fight took place with his sister Alycia at the table, when Alycia forced Edan to show some manners toward me. Edan gruffly pushed his plate to one side, told Alycia to fuck off and ran outside screaming and saying he wanted to die.

These were very traumatic and unforeseen times for me. I had never experienced anything even remotely like this in Edan. Where was my compliant, fun, and sweet little boy who always smiled, and allowed me to shower him with kisses every single day?

I suddenly became very afraid for Edan's future.

Edan unable to pose for a photo without first blocking his ears]

Heartbreak

Nothing is as painful as emotional loss. And when it's the loss of a child, it is the worst pain.

I wasn't going to lose Edan in the way a parent loses a child to unforeseen death or a devious ex-partner. My loss was about the control I'd had over a child I parented our entire lives; a child I reared through difficult times, whose disability I understood better than anyone.

My sense of loss had nothing to do with my ex-husband finally getting Edan full time. I simply didn't believe he could provide the attention to detail I bestowed on Edan. The Asperger's syndrome meant that Edan had to be guided through every inch of his life's routines, especially now that he was a hormonal, rebellious teenager.

I was never going to give Adam up. Adam's pure, unconditional love saved me, but what I would do was try to jump through every hoop available in order to keep Edan with us in Adelaide.

Through an old school friend of mine who has devoted her professional life to ASD, after her own son was diagnosed with it, we heard of Dr Tony Attwood, an English psychologist who now lives in Queensland and is an international authority on Asperger's syndrome. Tony was conducting a seminar in Adelaide in July 2012. Adam and I signed up for this immediately.

In the meantime, I posted a question online, in order to gain a broader perspective on queries I had about various issues.

I received two answers, but only one of them shone like a bright beacon, from a respondent named Nicholas.

This was my question:

I want to hear from anyone who has the Autism Spectrum Disorder, and how you see the world and people?

My 16-year-old son is on the more extreme end of ASD as an Aspie, and life is getting more difficult by the minute. I want to understand the mind and perspective of other Aspies out there. PLEASE HELP!

Nicholas' Answer

All of us are different. ASD is a spectrum, I have attributes of the syndrome your son doesn't have, he has some I don't have, and we may have things in common.

Of course, one of the hallmarks of ASD is difficulty in social situations and personal relationships. I've gone my entire life (56 years) with no close friends. I've even had trouble being comfortable with my own family. As far as a love life, I have had one relationship last four years. The average for me is two years, and the average time between relationships is five years. Until recently, I've never had a network or safety net of people to help me in personal emergencies. I have problems finding common threads with people, and I can't relate to most of what others talk about.

At gatherings, I'm always to the side or behind, or up against the wall away from the main centre of people. My social modus operandi is to make sure I'm always drinking or eating something—that way I'm not obligated to engage in conversation. I can't do small talk and because of my many sensory problems, I easily lose the flow of conversation.

Speaking for myself, over the years, I've developed a strong feeling of misanthropy. I realize I need people but I pursue my own interests and life.

Another point of ASD is sensory. Is your son overwhelmed by sound? Light? Changes in air pressure? Food tastes or textures? The feel of clothing? The smell of soaps, deodorants, laundry products? These are all a huge distraction. ASD's focus on the physical stimuli before hearing a person talking directly at us. We have no filters to eliminate the onslaught of stimulus—it all comes at us all at once. All or any one aspect may make an Aspie physically ill. We'll try desperately to escape a situation so as not to meltdown from overexposure.

Does any of this relate back to your son? Please elaborate in a follow up or we'll all answer in (typical for us) overkill. :D

I then replied to Nicholas, thanking him for his valuable insight:

Thank you, Nicholas,

You are almost describing my son to a tee. At the moment, the worst trouble I am having with my son is that he will block his ears and completely avoid me and my fiancée because he says the tone of my voice and that of my fiancées when combined is unbearable. He wants to relocate to New South Wales now to be with his father, as he does not want to share our home with the 'two of us' anymore. I don't fully comprehend his reasoning, because at his father's house (which is much smaller than mine), there will be six people, including a two-year-old, all living in close proximity. He has also identified the fact that he does not want my fiancée to be seen as his father once we are married, and he does not like it when my fiancée tells my son what to do (but that is typical teenage stuff). My son has always avoided social settings and is very solitary. He has a strict aversion to some types of cheese and has fainted at the sight of this. He has a medical alert at school. He has recently stated that he cannot eat at the table with us because he hates the eating noises we make. He also does not want the TV on because the noises are unbearable, although he will watch a movie at the cinema or listen to his iPad with earphones, which I find confounding. There is a lot of grunting and Tourette-like noise and facial/hand grimaces, ticks, and clicks from him, especially when he is stressed out. There's more, but the rest is not as impactful as what I've outlined here.

Nicholas' further responses

It sounds like your son is looking for a quick escape from the sensory difficulties, thinking that Dad's place is more tolerable. I somewhat doubt he's really thought it through. It's funny; we often go one way or the other... either no planning ahead or hyper-researching every nanosecond of an upcoming change. Generally, we don't like surprises or things to go awry—we don't cope well with unforeseen changes.

Lol. Yes, he can tolerate certain sounds and loud ones at that! I can't stand wailing violins, but I can listen to Nine Inch Nails all day!

The other response read:

I have borderline Asperger's and have difficulty concentrating if there is any noise, no matter how little. Asperger's is like having an amplifier on one's entire nervous system. I discovered that I became less annoyed by noise after playing a particular computer game for 20 minutes per day

※ ※ ※ ※ ※

Angelica's Correspondence With Edan

I attempted to reason with Edan in every way possible. I explained to him that moving to his dad's wasn't the answer. He had so much going for him here with us, like school and Yanek, his best friend in the world. He had teachers he loved, a new job at the Springton general store, his own spacious bedroom, freedom in the country, and of course our undying love. I begged Edan to reconsider. I promised him Adam and I would do our bit if he would.

Again, I utilised the written word to get Edan to communicate his feelings to me. Below is a transcript of an email exchange where I put my questions in italics.

You said you liked your room.

I can take most of the stuff from my room to Dad's.

But when are you going to see me?

During every school holidays.

Will u miss me?

Yes.

But if you miss me why do u want to go?

Because Dad said when it was just me and him, he wishes I'd live with him forever, and he cried when I was going on the plane to Adelaide in the school holidays just before and that made me feel really sorry for him seeing that I hadn't lived with him for ages.

But what about when I cry when you leave me?

I would feel sorry for you just the same with Dad but it's difficult choosing out of two people who are sad for me but I think Dad is taking the most pressure by missing me right now so I at least need to live with him.

Okay but will you ever live with me again?

I choose to live with him just so I can make him happy forever. When Dad said that he wishes I would live with him forever it made me feel like I should do it, but I was thinking of living there until I get really old. But I don't think I could be happy just seeing you now and then for the rest of my life.

Is it because I'm marrying Adam? Is he the problem?

Ok, maybe, there is a little problem I have with him it's because when you marry him I will have this feeling that Adam is taking over to be my real father, only if I live with you any longer and I would rather hate that because I'm not used to big fat bald men that yell a lot even when I'm not making noises and Adam did tell me off quite a few times even before I had that noise habit which made me feel a bit uncomfortable, and Dad is a lot more calm now because as a real father I know he loves me a lot more than Adam does, because Dad always used to tell me that he loves me more than anyone else in the world and that he wouldn't let anyone hurt me and that is exactly what Adam did when he grabbed me real tight and slammed me against my shelf, and I bet if Dad ever found out about that my dad would have a huge go at Adam.

This simple exchange of feelings cut through me like a knife. Adam felt very sad as well. He hated being the reason my boy was going to leave me. Still, we tried to accommodate Edan, all the while remaining assertive about our requirements. We started by drawing up a list of rules each person in the home must abide by. Below are Adam's and mine for Edan

HOUSE RULES FOR EDAN

MORNING ROUTINE:
1) Out of bed at 7.00am
2) Get dressed, put your socks on, and BRUSH YOUR TEETH.
3) Have breakfast

BACK FROM SCHOOL:
1) Get out of your school uniform
2) Put your socks in the wash

EVENING ROUTINE:
1) Shower at 8.00pm
2) Do at least ONE hour homework
3) Bedtime at 10.00pm on schooldays, and at MIDNIGHT on the weekends.
4) BRUSH YOUR TEETH

BEHAVIOUR:

No Swearing

Think before you get angry or want to run away

When MUM is not home ADAM is in charge and if he asks you to help around the house you need to do what he tells you. Adam never asks you to do too much work and he always helps you.

House Rules for Edan

Edan's reply to this was as follows:

Rules For Parents
1. *Don't stop me from having fun too much.*
2. *Don't give out too much homework.*
3. *Don't always break into my room like you own the place.*
4. *Let me have more breaks during the days.*
5. *Have a little bit less anger in you.*

THAT'S ALL!

We also received a reply to some problem-solving strategies I posted for Edan. The title of these read:

How am I going to change and behave better to avoid consequences?

I'm going to be quieter and I'm going to do as I'm told. I'll get up when the alarm clock goes off and have breakfast. I'll spend time with my family more and do some of the chores from the chart to earn money and I'll soon stop blocking my ears when people are talking to me.

I'll try to avoid consequences by being on my best behaviour, and that is all the stuff that I just said. I'll start to show more respect and I'll look after myself properly and I'll answer people's questions in a normal way. I'm going to act more like a grown up and listen to what people say by communicating with my family a bit more.

I'm also going to start using my 'pardons' instead of 'what's' and I soon won't mind that mum makes those noises that I really didn't like her doing. I'm going to be putting up with people coughing and sneezing and burping in the future. I'm going to try to think about something else when stuff like that happens, and which I struggle with sometimes. I will change one day, but maybe not until a while. I can put up with it sometimes quite easily, but mostly it's a bit difficult and it gets on my nerves.

One day, I will manage to cope with things better and I will get used to hanging around some people, even if they burp. I would like to be a little more normal sooner or later and I will also change by doing less noises, so that I won't make anyone too mad. I will change by answering people properly and I will see if I can make not such a big deal of people coughing.

Nothing changed. Edan persisted as he was, and his ears remained closed.

Nicholas soon became an email and Facebook friend and confidant. I turned to him for advice about my precious boy, the boy I devoted my life to, hoping one day he'd be 'normal'—the boy I was now going to lose if I didn't find another way. Pangs of emotional agony shot through my psyche. I couldn't let Edan go, I just couldn't.

Emails Between Nicholas (Niko), Adam, And Me

To: Niko

From: Angelica

Hi Niko!

My Aspie, as you know, is my 16-year-old son, Edan. I would love to write our whole history together, but that's a project I'm working on for publication. I wonder whether you'd like to be a part of that?

Edan has never been a difficult boy to manage until recently. He's witnessed a lot of emotional dysfunction in his short years due to a disagreeable marriage with his father and lots of changes and separations. Only in recent times has he become quite unreachable though, ever since I announced my engagement to my fiancée. We live in South Australia, and he has now requested to go and live with his father in New South Wales. This has caused me a great deal of grief, as I have invested so much into my relationship with Edan. He will be relocating on the 23rd of December.

I have so many questions for you, Niko, but my head doesn't know where to go first. Edan's Asperger's is so different to another Aspie boy I know of a similar age, and also really different to people whose stories I've read. I understand now why it's called a 'spectrum'. I've arrived at the decision that if the spectrum is 10 for very mild, and 90 for severe, Edan is currently on 70 or thereabouts.

So tell me a little about you and your diagnosis, and as we progress with our emails, I can tell you more and more about Edan. He was diagnosed at three years of age.

To: Angelica

From: Niko

Hi, Angelica

I was diagnosed about 4 years ago, at age 52.

I speak from my personal experience dealing with ASD. Hopefully having another Aspie's view may add to your own knowledge base.

Niko

To: Adam

From: Angelica

Hey bubba!

If you're bored and looking for something to do, how about you write a list of 'disorders' you have witnessed in Edan and their mitigating circumstances for me to pass on to Niko (my new Asperger's friend)

Thanks... have a great night, love you!!!!!!!!!!!!!!!!!!

To: Niko

From: Adam

Hi there, Niko,

I guess the thing I find most difficult about Edan is his noises and mannerisms. Since his diagnosis he has had a variety of tics which he replaces periodically. These can either get worse or milder, but they are always repetitive. Noises, face pulling, clicking, clapping, body twitches, and a complete aversion to certain sounds or words. He hates singing but accepts whistling. He cannot eat with us any longer because of our 'eating noises'. He will not speak to us if both of us are in the room and the TV is going because the noises are too bad, but will endure this at his father's.

At school, and at his part-time job, he is reported to be functioning and well-behaved. At home, it all goes to shit the second he steps onto the driveway. He now walks around with his fingers in his ears in order to shut us out. He is beginning to demonstrate aggression and increased isolation, which he claims to enjoy.

This is just the latest.

Not to mention the fact that he hates me 'yelling' at him, when in fact because he has fingers folding his ears down that he can't hear a thing, and I have to raise my voice!!! Then, on top of that, he has these outbursts where he literally chases you around the house, ears covered, shouting 'what, what, what' or 'mum, mum, mum' until he is answered on his terms, and then he can still ignore you!

Any thoughts?

Adam

From: Niko

To: Adam

Some Auties do make random sounds, but has Edan been evaluated for Tourette's syndrome? I'm not an expert on the condition by any means, but from my reading

(Oliver Sacks et al) it can get worse as one ages. Some meds can either dampen or worsen the symptoms. I don't know how common it is, but Tourette's and Asperger's can occur together.

The aggression or extreme, sudden anger I can really relate to. For you, it seems to come out of nowhere. Auties seem to have a short fuse. We do try to control our reactions, corking the bottle, so-to-speak, but we're easily pushed over the edge by the last straw. That can be anything from a noise, lights, smells, or someone's voice. That's probably one of the reasons why Edan's isolating. Understandably, he prefers isolation to over-stimulation and possible meltdown. Isolating helps him feel in control. To you, his isolation appears to be alarming. For Auties, it's pure heaven.

BTW, depression causes anger and aggression too. Has he been evaluated for that?

My anger manifests itself in either yelling or throwing things.

I'm the sole caregiver to my elderly mother. She has no understanding of the nature of Asperger's and thinks I can 'cure' myself. So my frustration at her reactions to my behaviours can throw me into a verbal tail-spin: physical violence, never.

However, if an object or machine doesn't won't work properly, I'm very methodical. I remove any salvageable parts, and then THROW that thing as hard as I can. The last one was a wonky lawn trimmer I threw 50 feet across the yard—quite an accomplishment for a skinny little guy. It was quite gratifying to have it smeared across the driveway. It was a "feels the power of Asperger's" moment.

I'm not sure of the mechanism that keeps us under control under certain circumstances. Edan's OK at work and school... it could be a matter of focus. Does he have a special interest he indulges in during his isolation at home? Immersing himself would help distract him. However, take care not to interrupt that time he needs for himself. We don't tolerate even simple intrusions if we're deep into something. It breaks our concentration, and with Auties, getting back into the mojo is long and difficult—especially for those of us who obsess over the passing of time.

Summing up, for Auties, isolation is a good thing.

Anger and aggression, though, need to be dealt with on some level.

Can you sit down with Edan and talk about accommodations to make him and you feel more comfortable? Right now all of you are walking on eggshells, waiting for the next reaction.

Maybe both of you can draw up a short list of 'grievances' and address them. Keep Edan to a 3 or 4-point list to start with, or the Aspie in him will overkill the assignment. He'll go overboard anyway, because naturally one thing will lead to another. If Edan can't talk about his feelings and what makes him angry, maybe he can go off and write it down or even draw it—sometimes verbal communication stymies us.

I should add, about my writing... Sometimes my brain and typing fingers miss a beat. So if you're reading along and see something odd, you may have to read around it to get what I really mean.

Niko

From: Niko

To: Angelica

Hi Angelica,

Tho' you've probably already guessed — I've never married nor had children, tho' I do have two grown nephews. The younger is NT, the older has some qualities of ASD.

Still, even with my lack of dealing with kids, we'll see what revelations we can kick up, and you can apply them to your experience. :)

At 16, along with ASD, Edan has the additional distraction of being a teenager. I know, I am stating the obvious.

How is Edan's behaviour at school and with the family? A girlfriend? How are his studies? In your perception, is his maturity level typical of a 16-year-old or, in many ways, does he seem younger?

I was maddeningly withdrawn as a kid and far into adulthood. At school, I lacked focus. I'm not sure if I had a learning disability — but looking back, it seemed like ADHD. Then, not being able to filter out distractions, I'd miss most of my class lessons and go winging off in odd directions when given an assignment — I made up my own rules for every subject. Yet, I could focus down on a detailed drawing and do fine pencil work for hours, day after day. I think at age 16, my maturity level was around 9. Now, I'm probably stuck at around 18.

Aww, too bad Edan has decided to leave for Dad's. Assure him that your door is always open for him to return if things don't work out. ASDs tend to have a problem recognising our own mistakes — though we have no hesitation in exposing others! LOL It's not so much a matter of ego or who's right — it's more like correcting the flow of knowledge. When we do perceive ourselves as wrong, it's mentally damaging. We ruminate on ours' and others' wrongs against us for years or even lifetimes. Chronic depression is common in ASDs.

My diagnosis... Over the years, I'd had an idea that I was different. But growing up the only definition I had was autism or, as kids in school called me, retard.

These last four years have been a juggernaut of internet surfing, learning most of the angles of me. "Most" because I think "all" would imply that I'm finished. Hardly farther from the truth, I'm a work in progress. ;)

You have lots of questions, eh? Let them flow and we'll see where it leads.

Later,

Niko

From: Angelica

To: Niko

I think you're brilliant! Life is difficult enough as a neurotypical, so imagine it for someone like you? Social norms are either black or white nowadays... you're either team A or B, forget about all the colours of the spectrum (no pun intended) or the rest of the alphabet! Modern philosophy would like to make one believe we are freer than ever but I do not think so. I've never felt as imprisoned as I feel today.

I've self-diagnosed Edan as having Tourette's. He is currently on 1mg of Risperidone, which has significantly subdued the noises. I don't know whether his father will continue with the treatment once he goes to Sydney, but that's totally up to him as Edan's full time caregiver now. I can only make recommendations and need to give up the control factor. Not easy for a staunch Taurean. What star sign are you?

I have read so much about ASD but your experiences, and Tony Attwood's (I went to his seminar recently) are the ones that resonate what is going on with Edan the most. I am aware of both the aggressive streak (frustration - and don't we ALL have it?) and the depression factors. I worry more about the depression. Could it lead to suicidal ideation? I don't know what your thoughts are on spirituality, but I am a great believer. I saw a clairvoyant not so long ago who said Edan's social contact would emerge once he went to live with his dad, and that she could see him hanging around a group of boys and even smoking! You asked me previously what age I think Edan might be intellectually, and I think 9 or 10 might be it. It's hard to tell due to the fact that Edan is not social and sociability is such a ruling factor in emotional maturity.

When I cannot reach Edan verbally, I often get him to write his thoughts down for me. As you can imagine, they are very literal and very one dimensional, but at least I know how he thinks. Up to very recently I worried that his consistent self-imposed solitude was damaging his psyche, until for the tenth time, Edan assured me it made him happy to be alone. And now YOU have verified this. Thank you. I guess I'm narcissistic, in that I want to know my son loves me. He says he does, but of course his actions (or lack of them) speak otherwise and so I'm left with a big empty hole inside. Can you shed some light on Aspies' ability to love and how they might show it?

I want to thank you for the trouble you are taking in responding to me. I greatly appreciate this and I love how you write.

So where do you live? And are you Italian? I'm half-Italian.

Angelica :-)

From Niko

To: Angelica

Hey! Of course Edan loves you!

Auties tend to be either aloof or over the top about expressing affection. I gather Edan's aloof, but don't equate his actions as an Aspie to what he feels in his heart. Often it's the pure expression that eludes us. Yep, a bad reaction can come off as being hurtful — for one thing, remember, he's a teenager! He's ALL about saying and doing things without really thinking them out. Then, put ASD into mix. We can't control how we react to the stimulus around us. I say that with a grain of salt. Some things we can learn around our neurological differences. It all depends on the levels of spectrum each of us was dealt.

For an Aspie, love and caring can be expressed in simple and/or odd ways. Edan may think writing down his communications to you is an act of love. He may not say "I love you" but, in his mind, he took the time and poured his heart out in the writing.

With us, Angelica, you have to turn your brain upside down, inside-out, and backwards. You have to do a lot of reading between the lines. Oddly, reading between the lines is something many of us Auties can't do! :D

I read Tony's book right after I was evaluated. Found it depressing, and of course, overly clinical in places. Reading some of the personal passages he culled from his interviews, I saw myself over and over again.

Oh man, the gorilla in the room: suicide. Is it part of the spectrum? I'll tell ya, it's a mixed bag from the others I've spoken with. I can only relate it to me.

I've been clinically depressed since I hit my teens. That included thinking of all the ways I could do away with myself. Aspie; bullied at school, at work, and primarily by Dad and by a much lesser degree, my Mom. They didn't know how to deal with me. Teachers and parents didn't know how to deal with a high-functioning, yet somehow, emotionally stunted kid in the 1960-70s. We're the ones who were called all the nasty names. There's a whole ocean of us out there who are only now getting a clue as to what makes us US.

What saved me? Not believing in a god or heaven. I figure this is THE only life I have — why waste it? I could either live, suffer, and enjoy fleeting happiness or be worm food in the grave. In my logical brain it was an easy choice — but I have to say, it took many years to finally see it this way. Oddly, no one's ever asked me if I were depressed.

When you read Edan's stuff, what do you mean he writes one-dimensionally? I think I know what you're saying, but I'm not sure.

OK more junk about me...

I'm a typical Libra. I usually see and consider at least two sides before making decisions — that's IF the two sides are obvious to me. Sometimes I have trouble seeing the big picture.

I'm an Italian wannabe. LOL

My background is mostly Slovak and Croatian. My joke is that my ancestors lived between the two greatest civilisations — the Greeks and the Romans — and somehow managed not to absorb any aspect of either. We were the barbarians who merrily joined the Mongol horde to burn the great, ancient libraries.

I live in Colorado, USA. I'm big on hiking and backpacking into the wilderness.

That brings me your next question ... If there is such a thing, I'd be a card-carrying atheist. I believe in hard science. However, I do entertain theoretical physics. I'm a nature "worshipper". My big love is ornithology — birdwatching. I can ID species on the fly. Botany, I take pictures ad nauseam, and then go to the books or internet for ID. Finally, geology, I love it, but I'm not great at it.

Niko

From: Angelica

To: Adam

I LOVE THIS GUY!

(By this stage Niko was my best friend in the world, so yes, I did!)

From: Angelica

To: Niko

The more I read about you the more I find I have more in common with you than 98% of neurotypicals! I actually don't think I'm an NT, my life has not allowed me to be. My autobiography is about this.

Well, all I can say is thank you for finding me. Personally I have always wanted to visit Colorado, so who knows... one day I might say 'hi' in person! I'm very touchy feely so expect a big hug! My son, of course, finds hugging difficult, and whenever I jump one on him, it's like hugging a cardboard cut-out, but I tell him to get over it and squeeze harder. It hasn't been as tense lately I must admit... at one point I couldn't even brush past him without him freaking out! I even planted a kiss on his cheek the other day without repercussions. I'm going to miss him so much!

Can I ask your view on Aspies and hygiene? Edan is not a fan of cleanliness and a lot of our wars are over this!

From: Niko

To: Angelica

You can pretty much ask me anything, Angelica. I'm an open book, perhaps with a few dog-eared or torn pages. :)

Personal hygiene. Great subject! I know you've read that, in general, both male and female Aspies don't give a damn about appearance. Fashion is not our thing. Cleanliness, though: I've heard that NT teenage boys have an aversion to cleanliness — not just for the rebellion aspect, but because they actually like their own odour. That's pretty high on the "uck" scale.

I've always been a clean-nic, not obsessively so, but being clean is calming to me. Any odour is a sensory problem. I'm very sensitive to the smell of personal products. I have to use all unscented, everything from laundry detergent and softeners, to soaps, lotions, and deodorants. So, here's my take — maybe Edan's sensitive too, and thus, refuses to use things that trigger him, right down to the clean, spring fresh towels and the clothing he wears. Really, it could be an issue that seems so small. The texture of the towels or his clean clothes against his skin. Even the sound — soft towels or clothing sounds different against the skin than stiff ones dried outside (think a fingernail on chalk board).

Is your water hard or soft? Soft feels slimy.

It all sounds picky to an NT, but, again, we can't help it. What may simply bug you can be a major physical and/or mental disturbance to us — in other words, meltdown fodder.

It took me a long time to really corner my "Aspie-isms". The things I won't put up and the things I will grudgingly tolerate. Could it be that Edan is unaware of many of the things that really get at him? Once in a while, I still discover some odd thing that makes me reassess. The latest are the eating utensils. I've been tossing the utensils with a design on the handle into the back of the drawer. I can't stand the tactile of my spoons, forks, and knifes that have decoration.

I'm calling it a day. Good morning to you and good night to me. ZZZzzzzz

Niko

Xoxo

From Angelica

To: Niko

Hi Niko,

Hoping you slept well. I am certain that Edan identifies his likes and dislikes. It's communicating these effectively to US that is the problem! And if he could, it would avoid so much friction... but.

The more you explain things, the better I make sense of them.

Tell me about sexuality. Edan is showing no interest in sex (that we know of) or future relationships, something that as a 16 year old is also expected?

From: Niko

To: Angelica

snicker

S. E. X.

About the best I can give you are my own experiences. So here's me...

Most of my adult life I tried to be other's definition of "normal", i.e. NT. I dated here and there, but mostly I avoided it.

First thing, I have to qualify: I enjoy hugging people well known to me, on a relative-to-relative or friend-to-friend basis. However, I didn't enjoy the hugging and kissing on the dating level. The simple touching I thought was gross. The mental stress to hug and kiss was painful. It's difficult to explain... A heightened sense of personal space is a typical Aspie trait. Someone coming in too close raises the hairs on the back of my neck and kicks in the fight or flight instinct.

Angelica, I didn't lose my virginity until I was 32! It was more of an Aspie logic thing than an attraction or sexual thing. I thought it was about time. I didn't enjoy it — and the two other experiments through the years also proved to be unenjoyable. On my level of Aspie logic, both physically and emotionally, sex is unnecessary for me.

Almost 13 years since my last relationship, I'm at a place where I just don't want to be bothered. People are just eye candy. I don't want relationships beyond my hiking buddies and I keep a few bends in the trail away from them. LOL

Niko

From: Angelica

To: Niko

Relationships are overrated. I truly believe we are transient beings who leave footprints wherever the need or mood takes us. Your hiking buddies are probably more satisfying to you than any romantic relationship. Romance is conditional and demanding and I, for one, have been a victim of it many times, until now.

You know, I really like how you think. To me, you are closer to spirit than most people I've met. I hope we can continue our uncommon dialogue for many days to come.

Angelica)0(

And yes, there were many more of these uncommon dialogues with Niko Gambeli, and I enjoyed each thoroughly. Asperger's syndrome or not, we shared a similar understanding of life and emotion.

Edan often came up with some perfectly lucid and logical arguments, which left me stunned.

It is important to understand that Asperger's syndrome sufferers have normal intelligence. In fact, many are savants in one area or more. Asperger's syndrome is merely a socially dysfunctional condition.

One of Edan's less graphic 'pornographic' cartoons about two boys at school

The Tony Attwood/Michelle Garnett seminar was a final godsend into the ongoing research on my son, as were two books I read simultaneously: Mark Haddon's *The Curious Incident of the Dog in the Nighttime*,[1] now a stage adaptation; and Megan Hammond's autobiography *My Life with Asperger's*.[2]

I was resigning myself to the fact that Edan was always going to be like this, that I had to give in to his wishes, because Asperger's syndrome was a very single-minded condition that did not lend itself to others' will. Tony called this inherent stubbornness, '*The God Syndrome*'— behaviour which described Edan succinctly. In fact, everything Tony and Michelle spoke of that day was 100% Edan. My neck grew stiff from the constant nodding in acknowledgement. No one and nothing quite captured the essence of Edan as much as did this seminar.

Edan *always* had to have the last word, no matter what the talk was about. Edan had to win at *every* game played. Edan was *always* right, and where moving back to Sydney and living with his father was concerned, there was no rhyme or reason that would sway his mind.

I was going to lose my Edan, and it hurt so badly.

Long after I left corrections, I decided to give the disabilities sector a go, in order to understand this area better. It was a mistake. There had been too many disabled people in my life already. I lasted one-and-a-half years with the organisation before leaving suddenly, feeling emotionally raw and with my nerves in knots. I had no job to go to.

That's when I decided to write this book.

One of my disability support work clients was a seventeen-year-old boy I'll call James. He not only had Asperger's but also had body dysmorphia. Many of the behaviours that James displayed were quite different from Edan's, and yet there were also some similarities.

James was obsessive about his appearance, sporting many looks and fashions ranging from 1930's chic, complete with walking cane and smoking pipe, to One Direction boy wear. No two looks were ever the same. Sometimes he wore make-up, other times he'd slick his hair in styles that 80's aficionados out there must be envious of. And there was always lots of jewellery.

James was a hoarder. He had umpteen pairs of shoes to go with every one of his many Walter Mitty outfits, and enough beauty products to make Helena Rubenstein feel deprived. I supported James in his own house, and it was hell

---

[1] *The Curious Incident of the Dog in the Nighttime*, Mark Haddon, Red Fox, 2014

[2] *My Life with Asperger's – The disorder that dominated one woman's life until she was diagnosed at the age of 26*, Megan Hammond, New Holland, 2011

trying to keep the place clean and tidy, let alone his overflowing room. Like Edan, James had to be asked to wash and change his underwear. The other clients sometimes complained that James smelled bad. He would pee all over his toilet, and take food into the lounge, which was constantly grubby.

James fancied himself an expert in all things, whether a protégée of Arnold Schwarzenegger with his bodybuilding or the next MasterChef champion.

James attended TAFE, studying hospitality and cooking. He failed miserably, because he had such a short attention span. He also chose not to revise the modules at home and yet he would tell the world he passed with flying colours and was the best student in the class. I remember sitting with James and his lecturer one afternoon as the staff member pounded James with reasons why he was not going to pass the course. James' tears ran down his face as he tried to convince the teacher that he was wrong, because James was the best student he had. In his own mind, James was indeed the best! It was everyone else who was wrong or could not see his amazing talent. James' *God Syndrome* was the most pronounced and omnipotent I'd have ever seen in *any* person, neurotypical or otherwise.

James had a very sinister streak in him, something that to date does not exist in Edan. This streak, which surfaced on many occasions, is the reason I asked to be excused from working with him. Having worked with teenage detainees, I have seen all manner of psychosis, from post-traumatic stress to drug-induced. Whenever James would go into one of his conscious flights of fancy, or if he became agitated (usually when denied a request or when reprimanded), his eyes would glaze over and roll back into his head.

James, unlike Edan, wanted a girlfriend and a sexual relationship. He attempted to fulfil this fantasy by accosting female staff in a highly calculated, strategic way. I did twenty-four hour sleepover shifts with James, and far too often I felt like the mouse inside a snake's lair. It was both frightening and nauseating. James would boast that every female in the Barossa Valley wanted to sleep with him. He became the reason some female staff left the organisation and, as his aggression escalated, he was eventually only placed with male staff.

James was the greatest mimic I've ever known. To the untrained eye, a lot of the time, James would pass as normal. He was a great conversationalist, well-informed on a variety of topics, an apparent extrovert, polite, charming, humorous (although very mechanical and contrived with his deliveries), and willing to try most things in life. He was also a consummate poet who could give Keats a run for his money. Behind closed doors, however, James was a terrifying monster, a pathological liar, and a ticking time bomb.

Like Edan, James had no real understanding of time, monetary value, or social etiquette. He constantly faked it till he made it. Like Edan, he could be incredibly logical and eloquent, and then so completely offbeat that it was painful. When I first met James, I asked myself, *'What Asperger's? If only Edan was more like him!'* When I stopped working with James, I was so pleased that Edan was nothing like him in the core areas that counted.

There are a lot of people just like James in prison.

Only days before Edan left my home on the 23rd of December, 2012, I was driving three of my clients to a destination in the beautiful Barossa Valley when a song by 'The Voice Australia' singing sensation, Karise Eden, came on the radio. The song is called *You Won't Let Me*, by Rachel Yamagata and Mike Viola.

The words cut through me like a knife and I couldn't contain my pain any longer. I broke down in a torrent of tears, much to my poor clients' concerns and kind but useless comforting. I was totally heartbroken, more so than from any failed romantic relationship I'd had.

> *"If you'd only let me,*
> *I could show you how to love.*
> *Take our time, let it all go.*
> *And if you'd only let me,*
> *I could show you how to cry.*
> *In your darkest hour*
> *I would lead you through the fire.*
> *But you won't let me, you won't let me."*

Our last days together, and Edan still hated me touching him

From Tony Attwood's seminar, where we bought his exceptional book (autographed as well!) *The Complete Guide to Asperger's Syndrome*, we learned more about a drug called Risperidone. Risperidone is sometimes used by ASD sufferers, to tone down some of their obsessive-compulsive behaviours.

I had always resisted placing Edan on medication, but having fought so many small battles and lost, I decided to give Risperidone a go. Edan responded very well to it, and it created some respite for both him and us. The tics, echolalia, rigid body contortions, and all-night pilgrimages reduced significantly. I was fairly certain Edan had some form of Tourette's, and Risperidone was instrumental with toning down the Tourette's symptoms to a minimum.

Had we discovered Risperidone earlier, perhaps Edan would not be leaving us, but that's life, and it is what it is. It was also a big lesson for me, in that I was shown I could not completely control the mind and will of another individual—Asperger's syndrome or not.

It took me three months of almost constant crying and the deepest heartache before I became used to not having my noisy, disruptive, but completely adorable boy around each day.

Sixteen years of trying to cure Asperger's, but now I loved Edan and accepted him all the more for it.

You really never *do* appreciate what you have until it's gone, do you?

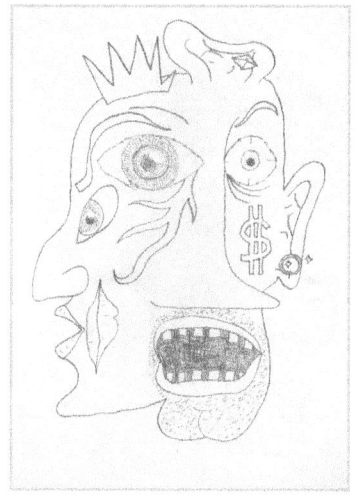

Edan's art

PART TWO
Edan's Edan

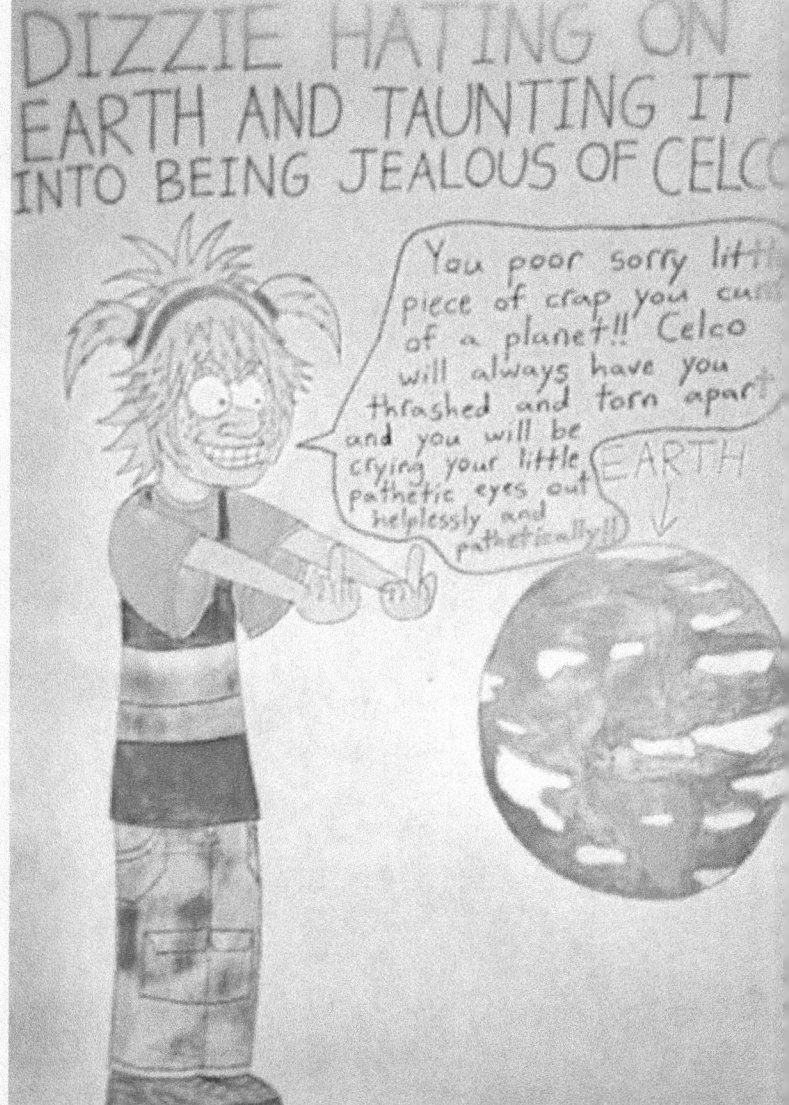

15 TO 17 YEARS OF AGE

The following anecdotes have been written *exactly* the way Edan wrote them. The only alterations made have been some spelling mistakes and punctuation. The art pieces are all Edan originals.

Asperger's

Asperger's is something that people have stuck in them.

I think people who have Asperger's are special people because there are not that many people in the world that have Asperger's.

Asperger's is like people who are really friendly and also have some good habits and bad habits.

Work

What I feel about work is not that good. Work is tiring and boring and hard, and it usually comes when you don't expect it, and that's why I don't really want to work.

This is my feeling about work.

Consequences

Consequences are something you don't want to get into. I think consequences means serious trouble that you can get into by doing something inappropriate and it also means punishment and getting grounded.

Consequences also mean no dessert and doing chores.

God

God is a man who makes people's life easier, and he would no longer be a mystery for everyone who knows what he looks like now.

God can create many things; he can show you the past and the future. God happens to know everything.

God is a powerful spirit high up in the sky.

Sex

I think sex means something that people do as a job in order to make a baby and that it's also a very strange way that women and men touch each other when it's making them want to keep doing it because they like it.

*A greater pornographic depiction of what may be
Edan's homosexual perception of two classmates*

Family

I think family is an important thing and caring thing and it's mainly full of love.

Family helps you get on with things easier, and I think that family does fight a lot of times and I also think family makes life a lot easier too.

Family shows a lot of respect to each other. And that's what I feel about FAMILY!! The End.

The word 'semen' in these drawings is pronounced 'semmen', as in a baby way of saying seven

My Mum

Question: What is the best thing about your mum?

Question: What is the worst thing about your mum?

Mostly there are best things about my mum and things that are kind of not the worst but stuff she does that I'm not used to yet.

The best things about my mum is that she's friendly, she cooks really nice food, she likes to play-fight with me and she takes me and Adam to fun places. I'm not that used to her making high pitched noises and sneezing. That is all!

My mum is a neat writer and she's a good reader, that's one of the best things about her and also when she and I read the BFG together.

I wish that one day mum will take me overseas and I also wish that she'll play more games with me more often.

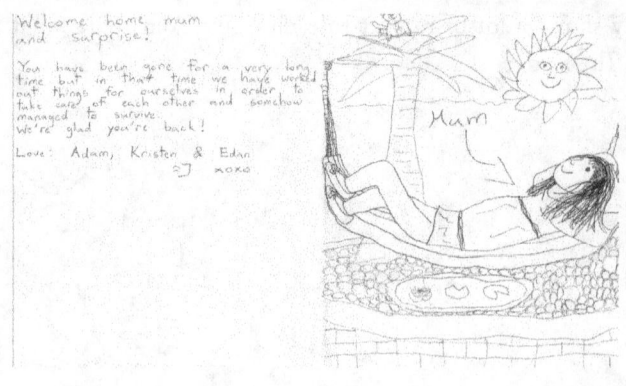

Edan depicted what he felt or witnessed about us in his hand-drawn greeting cards

My Dad

Question: What's good about your dad?

Question: What's not so good about your dad?

My dad is always good in my opinion. I don't really see him do things that are not good.

What's good about him, is even when he yells, he calms down very quickly and starts to talk softly.

When we go food shopping, he lets me get lots of food I want if I ask him and he likes to play murder in the dark which is a fun game.

Adam

I think Adam is okay. He's a little annoying but I find him a little friendly and he is not really fair most of the time, and he might have to do more exercise because he's pretty weak at the moment.

I'd say we get on just fine and he's a big help with some stuff and Adam is good at pulling weird faces. And that's how I feel about Adam Brewer. The End!!

My Sister Annabella

(This is Edan's third sister from his father's second marriage. Her name has been changed to protect her identity. Annabella was two at the time of writing).

I think Annabella is a gentle, friendly baby, I like her because she doesn't cry as noisily as most babies do and she's always nice and clean unlike other babies who poo and stink a lot.

What I also like about Annabella is that she can already run on bare feet even when she's still a baby and that she can also talk in proper words pretty early for a baby like her as well. And that is all what I think about Annabella.

Divorce

I think divorce isn't a good thing. I feel that divorcing happens to people a lot all over the world and it doesn't please the kids at all.

Divorce is when husbands and wives don't get along with each other at all and start to lose it. It makes the husband and wife feel very bad about themselves. It is not a fun thing. Even though I really think it is fun.

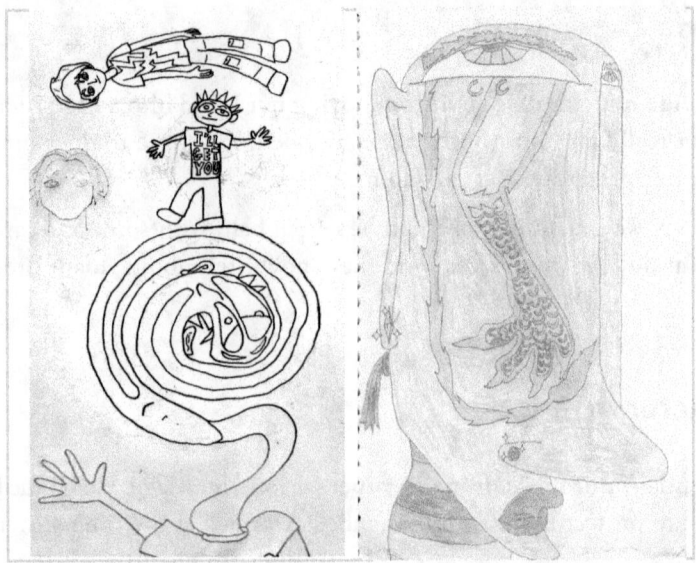

(Left) Every child's head spin, DIVORCE!
(Right) Maybe cubist artists were ASD too?

The Dark

I think the dark is so awesome. The dark is pitch black, and the dark happens in the night time too. I don't think the dark is scary, I'm not afraid of it and I can put up with the dark very well. I do believe that other people all around the world are afraid of the dark though, but there is no need to be scared of the dark, because the dark cannot harm you. It's always in your imagination when you think about things you're afraid of while you are in the dark.

Question: What is the purpose of people being on earth?

The purpose of people is that they can survive on Earth and they can help troubled people on Earth and the reason why people are in this world is because there are families and governments and people who look after animals and it makes the world a better place.

Also why people live in this world is because they want to go and learn at school and get smarter so they can get a job and earn money and they can use money to buy a house and to buy food and a car.

Why people live in this world is that there are also police, fire people and ambulances because they all help out other people, whether if there's a bad or drunk person, the police arrest them to make sure they don't hurt anyone or if anyone is in the middle of a burning building, the fire people come and rescue them or if someone is badly injured or really ill, the ambulance takes them to the hospital so they can get a lot better and look after themselves.

Edan hiding from the world of others.
"Maybe if I look like a frog in the grass no-one will see me?"

All about Edan by Edan

About me

I'm very funny and I like staying at home a lot all night and day. I laugh a lot. I'm a fast runner, I'm good at swimming, I'm good at climbing and I like playing football and I'm a fast eater and drinker. I always have the last say when I'm talking to people in a playing teasing way. My favourite food is McDonalds and I always feel proud of myself.

Edan – Year 7

Edan

I don't really remember that much about living in Auburn (spelled Orban) in Sydney when I was very young, but that's where I started off on the first day I was born. My mum was called Angelica and my dad was called B, and I noticed that all our surnames were called Galbraith. I also have 2 sisters, 1 called Alycia, who's the oldest and the other one called Kristen who's the second oldest, and later on in the future, I'm going to have a 3rd sister younger than me, but that didn't happen till ages away.

What I do remember is that we all moved to this house that was in a place called Gunn Place, St Helens Park in Campbelltown. I moved in a lot of different houses in Campbelltown and I remember there was one house we lived in the longest and I didn't think it was Gunn Place.

When mum and dad went to work a lot and as we all grew older, it was only me, Kristen and Alycia. Since Alycia is the oldest, she takes care of us, and we mostly just play games and watch TV, all 3 of us.

We had 2 cats for our pets, 1 was a grey and white cat called Tommy and the other was a black cat called Sebastian, they both died a while ago, but that's how life sometimes goes for animals.

Mum and dad were fighting a lot because of the "I want this and I want that and I don't want this and I don't want that," because of that type of argument. Once, they had this really big fight, they were slapping each other and stuff, and they got divorced. Dad went to live with his mum and dad W and L, which is our grandma and grandpa/nana and pop who we met a lot of times when mum and dad were still together.

Pop and nanna lived at R (suburb of Sydney) and so do my cousin, aunty and uncle. We also have another pop and nanna called Gloria and Alfio, who are mum's parents. Our uncle lives with Gloria and Alfio, and his name is Peter, but his parents call him Bimbo because he's not very smart and he's got a problem with his brain, and he sticks to being called Bimbo more than Peter. Uncle Peter is mum's brother too.

*The 'Shower Cap Patrol' – Edan, Alycia and Kristen.
When silliness was cohesive.*

Question: What kinds of things make you happy?

I like playing video games, watching my DVD's and jumping on the trampoline. I enjoy playing with my iPad and my DS. I like having alone time most of the time and I also like going out to places with just me and my mum.

I really like the High School I go to and I have fun going to my friend Yanek's house and I also have fun playing on the Springton oval and at the park next to the oval.

I like visiting my dad in Sydney and I enjoy getting take-away for dinner. I like sleeping in my own bed and Playing on the computer.

Question: What makes you the most afraid in life?

In life I get afraid of eating cheese because I think cheese is the worst food ever made. It doesn't taste very nice and it smells bad even more when someone's smelly breath is added to it. THAT'S ALL.

Question: Who are you?

Question: What do you want to do with your life?

Question: Who do you want to be?

I am normal and glad about myself, and I like having time to myself. I am someone who doesn't have any problems.

I want to have fun a lot with everything that I can think of what to do, and I also want to sleep in or get up very early a lot too.

What I would like to do with my life is to keep it the way it is right now and just have easy goings. I want to be a champion at video games and achieve something from it, and I would rather be a human.

Edan's take on Hermione, Harry and Ron on the megasketcher, circa 2003

Question: What do you want for Christmas (2011)?

A large box of favourites, Harry Potter and the Deathly Hallows part 1 and part 2 on Blu-ray DVD and an iPad number 2.

Question: If you wanted to run away, where would you go and what would you do?

I would try to earn some money from people and try to find a hotel to stay at and what I would do is try to earn some more money like doing chores for people at their house, so I can buy food to eat for dinner and lunch and breakfast.

When I'm a bit settled down, I'll go back home and give out a big apology to my parents for what I did that made me want to run away from home, and I will feel a lot better and will never do it again, ever. THE END!!

Edan drew Edvard Munch's 'The Scream' repeatedly for a period of time. It was only later in our lives that I understood the fascination with this picture. Edan was trying to cope with a noisy world, and often it made him scream!

Question: Why do you need to make noises all the time?

I like to make noises all the time because when other people make lots of noise, I like having the last little shout, and because it's something fun to do when there's really nothing else to do. I usually make those noises just to play around. And that's why I make noises all the time. THE END!

Thank God it was the last little shout, and not the last big bite like his friend behind him! Adelaide museum, circa 2010.

Question: Write down ten things that make you happy and ten that make you unhappy. Write ten things you like about you and five things you could change about you.

(This was written after Edan moved to Sydney.)

Ten things that make me happy

1. Living with my mum
2. Going to live with my dad
3. Spending time with my best friend Yanek
4. Playing video games
5. Having alone time
6. Going to school
7. Spending time with mum outside the house
8. Kristen coming over on the holidays
9. Working at the General Store
10. Giving out Christmas presents to people I like.

10 things that make me unhappy

1. People yelling at me
2. Not being able to see Yanek
3. Having too much hard work
4. Mum dying
5. Dad dying
6. Not getting any Christmas presents
7. People breaking into my house and stealing all of my items
8. Adam upsetting me
9. Neighbours talking too loud when I'm trying to sleep
10. Seeing my best friend getting bullied

10 things I like about me

1. I like that I'm good at spelling
2. I like that I have a best friend
3. I like that I'm good at maths
4. I like me having a good mother and father
5. I like that I'm kind
6. I like that I'm a hard working person
7. I like me earning so much money for my bank
8. I like that I'm good at video games
9. I like me being a teenager
10. I like that I'm good at art

5 things I wish I could change about myself

1. I could become less shy of people
2. I could not block my ears anymore and not repeat saying the same word over and over again
3. I could eat dinner inside the house with everyone else
4. I could get Facebook
5. I could learn how to drive a car in the age I'm in now.

Mum: "Edan, make a list of all the things you're going to take to Adelaide with you, and a list of the things you are going to leave behind here in Adelaide."

The list Edan made of the personal items he wanted to take back to Sydney when relocating to his father's

Watching Edan pack his things, and in many instances, having to pack them for him, was one of the hardest things I've ever had to do. I cried throughout the entire exercise. The emotional pain was incomparable.

Stories

My Bali Adventure

For my summer holiday, I travelled to Bali on a plane with my sister Alycia. It took a while to get there but we eventually got there, and when we arrived in Bali, I've noticed that it was really hot; everyone has different rules including the traffic. The buildings look like they're all ancient temples because there were strange statues everywhere, and there were lots of trees, it was nothing like Australia.

I had a very good time there but there was one thing that I didn't really like a part of Bali is you have to wear one of those Balinese necklaces with flowers, but the rest of the stuff there, I enjoyed a lot. I did all kinds of fun things in my first time in Bali. I went to Waterbomb Park, and what I did at Waterbomb Park, I went on the world's steepest water slide you could ever go on, and it was amazing, it was my first favourite water slide. It's where you stand on this shut lid that has a cross on it which means that you have to cross your legs and your arms as you're standing up and also putting your head back, and this machine is counting 3, 2, 1, and then that lid your standing on opens really fast and then you shoot right down like crazy, it was very exciting. I went on lots of other water slides like the Boomerang and Super Bowl water slides.

Next I went to Tree Top Adventure Park. I had a good time there too. I did all of the different challenges they set up for you to do. There was zip lining, net crossing, rope jumping, crawling through tunnels high off the ground and bridge crossing which was great fun, but Alycia was struggling with it but she was having fun too.

And that is it for my story about my holiday in Bali. The End.

Edan and Alycia in Bali. Edan was extremely unimpressed with having to wear a sarong in order to enter a temple. That umbrella connected quite harshly with a tree during a tantrum over this matter.

Tree Top Adventures. Edan is actually a very athletic boy with amazing muscle control

The story below was written when Edan was 11 years old. Jamie was my partner at the time, and Edan struggled with the concept of loving another male that was not his father, usually following any sign of physical or verbal affection with a proclamation that he was 'not gay'.

The 'pop' and 'nanna' he refers to here are his paternal grandparents. Pop died in 2005 and nanna suffered a massive stroke not long after, spending the rest of her life in a nursing home. Nanna suffered terribly with agoraphobia and various obsessive-compulsive disorders. Nanna died in 2013.

My Family

My family is the weirdest family I ever had.

Sometimes dad says or does stuff that you shouldn't be doing, but later on he says *do the stuff you shouldn't be doing*. Like what happened to my school, and my school is very stupid and crazy and I know I had a very good life when everything used to be normal, like what happened in a long time ago, when pop used to be alive and when nanna used to be out of the hospital and she used the torch and come to every door in the house and count. And like when pop used to watch the football and cricket, I had the best life time ever, but my life began to be worse like now and nanna's house used to be a bit new and how they had biscuits. They had everything different and I liked it that nanna cooks spaghetti bolognaise for dinner every time, and she makes this nice cup of tea.

I love my nanna and pop. I love my father. I love my mum. I love my two sisters and I love Jamie as a friend. Everything was different like it used to be.

Edan

(Top) Edan's perception on death was pretty much what he learned about it in scripture classes at school. In this picture before his pop died, these were the ones that passed away who were close to him, Tommy and Sebastian, our cats, Squeaky and Renee my daughter's pet mice, and Darcy, a family friend who succumbed to a brain tumour aged five. (Bottom) As Edan matured, so did his perceptions and skills.

My Year At School – Year 6

The work I did here was maths and G.L. and I work on cartoons like the Simpsons. We used dot points and questions about one episode of the Simpsons and we listen to some other kids do their cartoons and we watch their cartoons as well like Woody Woodpecker, Bugs Bunny, Tom And Jerry and even Inspector Gadget.

I go to the Wetlands with Mr B and all the class. In the Wetlands we water the vegetables with the watering can and pull up weeds and pick some mulberries from the tree. Parents can come to buy vegetables on Fridays. We planted a special Australian grapevine.

Nearly every day we do spelling practice and we have a test every week. I've been on two excursions since I've been here. The first excursion was when we went to Adelaide and went to the Botanical Gardens and went to Chinatown, it was fun.

My second excursion was Bolivar and we went to a big playground, it was fun. I did croqueting and learnt how to do the basic stitching. We do art and we can draw anything we want. I got to know all the kids and I play with them at lunch and recess and I really enjoy doing that.

We do PE and my favourite PE is hide and seek brandy, I used to like Flags. We go to the juniors sometimes and before school starts, and when we go to class we line up in a square like the juniors, Year sevens, Year sixes, Year fives, Year threes, and the Year fours. The principal stands at the front with her dog Gnasher and the teachers stand at the front too. We say good morning to the teachers and parents and nannas and pops and the really little dudes and dogs. The principal always says little dudes ready set go! Which means she lets the Year twos, Year ones and the Kindergarten go to class first and then we go to class and I got to know all of the teachers, one Mr B, two Mrs G.B., three Mr R, and four Mrs B. I got to know the library teacher, Mrs K, and her helper is Mrs R and I got to know her as well. And I got to know this other teacher that comes here usually whenever called Mr L, and my principal's name is Mrs B.K. and I got to know two teachers that came here once, one Mrs J. who teaches German like Mr R, and two, Mrs B. I had a great time here like I'm having now.

My Friendship with Yanek

I miss Yanek because he's funny, he's polite, he's easy to hang around with and he's never upset and always happy. I also miss him because of the good old times we had at Birdwood High School. We played football and basketball at lunch and recess and we always work together like mates.

When I was standing alone leaning on a pole during lunch and recess Pat found me and introduced me to Yanek. I then got joined in to be in the Special Ed classroom and so did Yanek, it was just only me and Yanek in this one classroom and Yanek had a disability just like me and then we became best friends because we got to know each other for when it was just me and him working in this small classroom called the Special Ed.

At school I enjoy talking to Yanek while working, playing PE with him and playing sports with him at lunch and recess. I enjoy going to the pools and the movies with Yanek and I also really enjoy going over to Yanek's place to sleep over and him coming to sleep over at my place. I also really like doing all sorts other things with Yanek like going to Mannum to do some fishing with Adam, going to the bakery for lunch, going bowling and do some golfing, playing with Gogo together and watching DVD's and playing video games together.

Edan's fanciful take on Yanek

Edan with his cousin's dog Jack on a sand dune in the Yorke Peninsula, a favourite spot for Edan when he first arrived in Adelaide in 2008

Silly Things

A collection of random notes Edan left for us to read:

To Mum!

Sorry, I couldn't finish the picture because I sort of wanted it to be perfect and I was spending a little bit of time with Alycia because I needed some breaks when I was drawing that picture because it's not easy like those cartoon drawings, the one I'm doing now is real life drawings by hand and everybody needs breaks when they're doing hard work drawings like that, it really hurts your hand and you need to give it a good shake and rub.

But this is at least what I done so far, hope it's still really good, and got a lot of smart ideas in it. I'll try very hard to finish it tomorrow and do as much as I possibly can. I did as much as I possibly could do today, but I hope you still like it.

I'm really sorry.

Edan

I don't care if people touch my neck and thrust, because it is not a private part and it is not a big deal if somebody touches it. If someone comes near me then I'm not going to move away because they want to show me love, not hurt me.

It is okay for people that I know to hug me and show me some love because that's what people do. I am a nice boy, I will do the same and act like a grown up from now on.

Edan

(Left) Another image straight from Edan's photographic imagination
(Right) Self-portrait

I love Mum with all my hearts, who loves Mum the most, me I do, I love it when Mum does funny things, I love it when Mum does magic tricks, she looks lovable and she is very, very, very nice to me the most.

I love her so much that I kiss her and hug her a lot. She smells nice and wonderful. So nice.

Love you,

From Edan

4th of September 2005.

*Queensland 1999.
I love the way Edan reaches out to my hands.*

There's too much rich and famous popular people living on the Earth so they have to get off it!!

The black snakes and hands with the ghosts need to get off the Earth!

The people who love the Earth so much and everyone else need to get off it! And they will punch the crying worms!

There are so many worms moving and crying under water in the bath and the pool with the black hands touching you under the water! And the worms are going to get you! And the black snakes are going to get you!

Too many light blue salt with light blue cashews so they need to get off the Earth!

Too much McDonalds so it needs to get off the Earth.

Ronald McDonald with the big black dick needs to get off the Earth!

No more Harry Potter cos it's too magical.

That's enough light blue salt with light blue cars and the cashews need to get off the Earth!

The cars are too comfortable so they need to get off!

The Earth with the Americans needs to get off it!

No people on the Earth cos we need to get off it.

(Top & Bottom) Edan is a master of detail

I already made half of my lunch so don't worry about putting the snacks in case I already did it and all you have to do is make my sandwich that's all you have to do, nothing else but to make my sandwich and even though

I already told you about that I just wanted to remind you again by writing all of this so have a goodnight Mum and Adam!

OGWADABWAH!

Formorboodas!

Skdudrairdro!

Equadoorzoor!

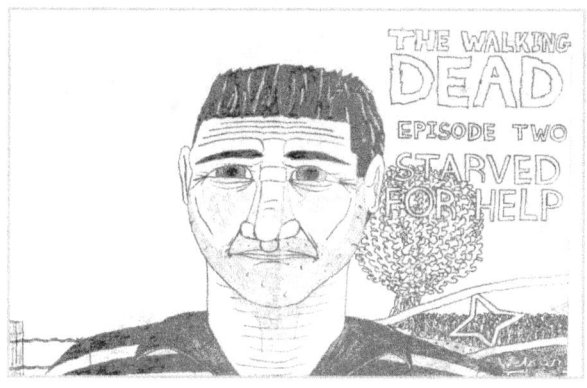

Edan's new obsession now is the American HBO series 'The Walking Dead', and his favourite character is The Governor. This picture was drawn just before he returned to Sydney.

PART THREE
Everyone else's Edan & other journeys

PAT'S EDAN

Hi there,

My name is Pat. I have been working with students who have special learning and complex needs for over 20 years now.

I love working with these special people, they have the most to give to our world but yet they are the most misunderstood humans on our planet. Our world has 'labels' on. They are doomed to a life to '*be seen and not heard*' and definitely, at all costs, '*keep them out of the public view*'. If you see them it is not encouraged to smile or provoke conversation and acknowledge that they too have rights. The right to participate, enjoy, share and have the same basic needs we all have… to be accepted and loved. But generation after generation continues to look upon them with dare I say it displeasure, fears and ignorance.

This is the fact, and I am just one of the many people who try to bring about acceptance and assist in breaking down the variety of barriers that exist for the families and the children that live with the many facets of 'disabilities'. In my job I get to not only work with the special young ones but get to know their families too. These families I have the deepest, deepest respect for because they allow me to share their lives and all the complexities they deal with. These families need support too in helping them reach what they see and deal with daily. They are special people in themselves, they have to brave the social stigmas, red tapes, ignorant and uninformed prejudices from the rest of the world and sometimes, painfully, from their own families.

Parents haven't been dealt a bad batch of luck in the form of a child with learning or complex needs, they haven't been bad or naughty to which the hand of God has swiped them with, they have a unique set of learning curves to start a life with…Hard yes, but any harder than watching your child grow into a beautiful young person only to have him taken away from you in an unfortunate incident? Leaving their precious one's brain damaged or wheelchair bound? I think not.

Some if not most of the times their children are totally unaware of the silent tears, the endless concerns and consistent sacrifices and extreme understanding that each parent and other siblings go through. But deep inside, they know the love and support they get from their families is the essential essence in them knowing and belonging. Hard to express? Yes. Hard to frequently verbalise or show it in other ways? Yes. But none the less, it is there.

I first met Edan Galbraith in 2010 at Birdwood High School while I was assigned to work with another student, both in their eighth year. Edan was not in our classes at the time but I soon noticed him…

Edan, on our way down from lesson this particular day, you caught my eye. There you were, pacing from one foot to the other whilst simultaneously springing your back off the pole on which you were leaning; in your hand was your lunch, your head was looking towards the sky, as if to reach for your last breath in a desperate attempt to keep your head above the water, but it wasn't water, it was a sea of noise, sounds and smells… an overload of sensory perceptions a nightmare for you. You were in one of the busiest areas of the school, the canteen area. My heart went out for you.

Every recess and lunch you were there in the same spot, same pole, repeating the same actions.

It took us, my allocated student and me, a little while to convince you to come and spend lunch with us for this meant change for you, and going to a place that you were not familiar with…

Yanek is the student I had been allocated to work with. Yanek, a student with complex needs and health care requirements, had the special provision of a small room that would accommodate for those needs and he also used the facilities there for his food requirements during his recess and lunchtime.

Yanek and Edan became and still are the best of buddies and that is an amazing story in itself.

That little space soon became a haven for all of us from the business and noise of the school day. When things got a little too much for him, when his senses would overload, Edan would just sit himself down in our little lounge area and rest and draw. He knew how to manage his 'disability' by his 'ability' to know when to withdraw and recoup.

There as time progressed, friendships and relationships grew. 'The boys' (as I will now refer to them) had a place where they could be themselves in a safe environment.

Edan is a great student to work with. He has so many talents and abilities it was a sheer pleasure to watch him grow, mature and develop in character. He is well liked amongst his classmates and independently developed relationships with other students who would allow him to be himself and express his quirky humour and antics. He is kind and sensitive and quite intelligent in his understanding of his environment and the world in which we all live.

He has an amazing ability for spelling words; he liked the challenge of tackling each new introduced word by breaking it down into its own syllables. Daily spelling tests became the opening of our days and we would all laugh and joke on each spelling achievement and the challenging words I would tempt each appetite with. I feel without a doubt that the best words ever would have to be 'Supercalifragilisticexpialidocious' and 'Antidisestablishmentarianism'. Sheer laughter and amazement for all involved on that day with Edan's achievement: it will ring in my ears and put a smile of my face every time I remember it.

Another of Edan's literacy achievements is his beautiful handwriting. Every word is perfectly unified in its lettering, correctly placed on the line with all I's dotted and T's crossed. He writes how he see's things…purely and truthfully.

Edan is a master of the pencil; pencil he writes and pencil he draws. His portrayal of third dimensional characters is an inspiration in itself. Once we became aware of this Edan was encouraged to join the same art class as his buddy Yanek and from there onwards even Edan became more aware that his ability to draw was a good thing to work on for himself also. After a little while of helping him overcome his inhibitions and try some new art techniques, it was breathtaking to watch him try new mediums, and experiment with different formats other that paper and pencils, although he worked slowly, the patience to wait for him to accomplish each task was always worth it.

We, the boys and I had lots of fun learning in our special area of the school. We would laugh and joke, playfully making fun of each other's quirky things we all do, but we also had precious times we shared with each other too…

Pottery high school project, which Edan gifted to his father

Like when Edan was upset about Adam's dad's passing. It struck a chord with Edan and he shared with me how he understood that loss.

We talked about how Adam was feeling and would feel as he grieved. Edan was concerned for Adam. We shared those moments of life that affect us all... life and death. The boys shared in my loss also, when my future son in law was killed in a motorbike accident.

We were class buddies, friends and a mateship grew between each and one of us.

My time at Birdwood High School will always hold such a special place in my heart of hearts, because I got to meet and got to know one amazing and very special young man... Edan Galbraith, who happened to have a label on him naming him "Asperger's", just as well as I don't see labels!

Pat's Edan. That lonely boy spending each school break leaning against a pole.

Kristen's Edan

One of Edan's most prominent characteristics was his ever-expanding list of self-created games. Many he played with himself, and many were shared with either, or both, me and my elder sister.

Most were simply just noises or made-up words that would go in the style of a tune or a repetitive manner that would make it unique in its own way. Some were a mix of English words that made no sense put together, and some were just his favourite things repeated in a song-like fashion (i.e. *Brown Custard*). These kinds of sayings would be used in a way for Edan to demonstrate excitement over something, or sometimes, used for anger. A lot of the time the speaking of the words would be combined with him clasping his hands together and making a cross-eyed face.

Edan used to like playing memory and snap a lot, as he was quite good at it, as well as being very competitive. I would let him win on occasion to lift his ego and make him feel proud of himself. It would be a game in itself to pretend to be stuck while playing a game or make an obvious wrong move, because you could see the rising excitement of him realising he will win, permeate across his face. When he did win, Edan would go into his champion ritual of clapping his hands and saying one of his unique phrases to himself in rejoicing.

Among these made-up games there were also more physical games. One was jumping on the trampoline together while singing a song about it. Another was sitting down outside with tea and biscuits commonly referred to as a "tea party".

A game he usually liked to play alone but sometimes would allow a second person to participate in was the re-enactment of scenes from his favourite movies, either with or without props. There were no toys for some of the less popular characters, and so Edan would make them himself. Such as the volleyball 'Wilson' from the movie *Cast Away*, with a face made from a bloody handprint. He simply got a similar looking ball from the back yard and drew the face on.

He also drew pictures on a paper and cut them out and talked to them, like *No-Face* from the animated film *Spirited Away*, which he placed on a tall stick. This one he was particularly obsessed with and would play with by himself for hours and which you could see the top of the head-on-a-stick from the side alley next to the back yard.

When he got older he was more into dressing up as his favourite characters as I suppose this gave him entitlement to their characteristics and he felt more realistic in them. He would often dress as Indiana Jones and even had the whip, gun, and hat to complete the outfit. Once he was so consumed in the character that he charted outside late at night while I thought he was upstairs. When I heard noises of someone walking around outside and turned all the lights off, I suspected a thief lurking and armed myself with a kitchen knife, only to be surprised to see Edan heroically standing under the garage fighting off imaginary villains.

Edan as Indy!

Because Edan and I are such movie/game buffs, we often in boredom play a game where we will say lines from a movie and the other has to guess where it's from. We also used to recite entire scripts from movies we would watch over and over again, and still often do. Now Edan is still into dressing up and collecting merchandise from his favourite franchises, and seems to tend towards characters that tend to have an evil mannerism or some sort of psychological or physical deformity. Edan has a very unique taste of what he finds enjoyable and fun, but then again, so does everyone.

Kristen's Edan. Jamberoo Recreational Park, NSW

Alycia As Watcher

A behavioural survey undertaken by Edan's eldest sister, Alycia. Edan is aged five.

Edan does *train* (or bus) with Kristen's clock for three minutes on Kristen's bed. He was also saying; "*Bus we at home? Yes, we're at home.*"

He then got the hiccups and said; "Alycia! I've got the hiccups!" I then asked him if he wanted breakfast now. He looked at the tin that had apples on it and said; "*No! I want Weetbix!*" Edan then did *train/bus* with Kristen's slip on shoes and made clicking noises.

Edan did *train/bus* and made different shapes with the shoes for another three minutes. He then went into his room and put his sandals on. He picked up Kristen's shoes and took them outside with him. Edan asked "*Where's Tommy and Sebastian?*" He played with Kristen's shoes for two minutes.

Edan walked down the side of the house and stopped half way and looked at the plant. He saw Tommy, and he followed him out and did *train* for one minute. He stopped and looked at the ground. Edan yelled; "*Alycia! Come and look at the caterpillar!*" I replied "*No*" and he said "*Caterpillar!*" He pointed to Tommy and said "*Pussycat! Not Tommy! Pussycat only! Two pussycats, grey one and black one!*"

Edan did *train/bus* for another four minutes. He stopped and then pretended Kristen's shoes were aeroplanes. He then spun around and did *train/bus* again. He then said; "*Come on! We are going to wait for the bus with the white door. Oh look! There's the bus with the white door!*"

Edan *train/bus* again for another three minutes and then comes inside. Dad asked Edan what he was doing. Edan put the two shoes down and took one step outside. Dad told Edan to come in and get dressed. Dad asked him for a kiss good morning but Edan refused. Dad asks him again and this time Edan says "*Yes! Kiss and cuddle!*" Edan gives dad a kiss and a cuddle and says; "*Daddy, have you got white undies?*" Dad replies "Yes."

Edan gets the two pink drum sticks and did *train* with them. He starts running around the pool table with them following the music on the TV. Dad calls him and Edan goes to him and says; "*I'm coming!*" Edan asks Dad again if he is wearing white undies. He then sees the racing car in the toy room and he says; "*Is that the racing car in Warwick's house?*" six times.

I stopped watching Edan at 10.16am

Toddler Edan inside Tommy and Sebastian's house, NSW

Yanek's Edan

To my best friend EDAN.

The first time EDAN and I met it was when EDAN was standing near a pole and then I came up to him and cheered him up by talking to each other and making jokes as well.

From the time EDAN and I met our friendship has grown stronger every year.

We had good times and bad times too but now we are more than just friends we are best buddies and we both make each other laugh.

Every time I see EDAN leave to go to Sydney I sometimes feel sad because I always say to my self EDAN please came back to South Australia.

Every time in the holidays I go to EDAN's house to sleep over then EDAN comes over to sleep at my house. EDAN you helped me at high school and I also helped you too because best buddies never give up on each other.

The best thing about EDAN is that he's funny, nice, and sweet, talks a lot, is a fast runner, does sport, works, and likes computer games. I like EDAN because he's like a brother to me because we both help each other out through all the years and it means a lot to me.

EDAN and I do a lot of things like: play basketball, walk around Williamstown, going bowling, hanging out together, spending time together, talk a lot, fishing and playing games.

No one I like better than my best buddy EDAN GALBRAITH.

I miss you, buddy. From your best buddy YANEK RACHWAL.

PS... BEST BUDDY'S FOR LIFE!

Sabrina's Edan

Where to start with Edan? I have known Edan since he was four years old. We met because his eldest sister, Alycia and I attended the same school and discovered we were neighbours. Living across the road from each, meant we were at each other's house frequently. The Galbraiths soon became a second family to me.

One of the first memories I recall of Edan was when Alycia had invited me over to their house after school. I walked in to discover Edan hopping up and down, flapping his hands in the air and making strange noises. I found this a bit odd and asked "*Um Alycia, what's your brother doing?*" She replied "*Oh that's just Edan. He always does that.*" Curiously, I asked "*Why?*" Alycia laughed at my reaction and said "*Oh, 'cause he has Asperger's.*" Alycia attempted to explain to me what Asperger's was, as I had never heard of this condition before. Angelica later informed me all about Asperger's and how it affects Edan. From then on, each time I would visit the Galbraith's home I knew what to expect from Edan and soon became familiar with his behaviours.

We would play with Edan and even adopt some of his little quirks and rituals. I have very fond memories of our time spent with Edan. One of the funniest things we still joke about to this day is the word 'Semmen.' Edan had made this word up and had four actions to accompany it.

The actions of Semmen:

1. Hold pointer finger closely in front of your face, stare with great concentration until your eyes go cross-eyed, jump from your left to right foot and chant "Semmen! Semmen!"

2. Put both hands together in front of your face (palms facing you), separate hands about thirty centimetres apart, then put your head through the gap and say "Semmen!" Repeat this movement several times. This stemmed from Edan's fascination with train doors opening and closing and was his representation of this happening.

3. Take one of your hands, place the edge of your hand against your hipbone, move your hand against your hipbone in a back and forth motion and say "Semmen!" This was another fascination of Edan's when he noticed the imprint the elastic on his shorts left on his body. He liked the bumpy feeling the shorts imprinted on his skin.

4. Stand on both feet, hold both arms at head height with hands in a beak like shape, repeatedly hopping forward on one foot then lean over the mega sketcher while clicking your beak hands and call out "Semmen! Semmen!"

I also remember Edan being an amazing and talented young artist. He could draw picture after picture on his mega sketcher. Not only could Edan look at something and draw it, he was able to draw from memory. Even things that he had seen months prior. This is where the fourth action of Semen came into action. After each drawing Edan had finished, he would stand up and do this ritual.

Edan has now grown into a lovely young man. He still remembers all the fun times we had and continues to have his own little quirks and ways about him.

Edan has taught me that someone living with Asperger's may be a challenge at times for both the person as well as the family. I can only give credit to

Angelica, B, Alycia and Kristen for the way they have raised Edan and how well he has turned out. Thanks for all the fun times and…

SEMMEN!!!

(Left) Straight after the divorce with nw boyfriend, Nick (obscured), Sabrina (left), Angelica, Alycia, Kristen, and Edan. (Right) Sabrina Schwalger (third from left) doing the 'Number Semmen' actions with bride Angelica and bridesmaids, Kristen (far left) and Alycia (far right). Ten years later, Sabrina is still obsessed with Edan's baby idiosyncracies.

What Asperger's Syndrome Feels Like For Some People I Know Robbie Rogers

Our Autism Journey

My husband and I were so excited with the birth of our son Brad in 1996. Eighteen months later we were blessed again with our beautiful daughter, Emily. We were living in a small country town, our family was complete and life was good. Little did we know of the dramatic turn our lives were about to take. Our son Brad was a very unhappy baby. He cried most of the time and nothing seemed to comfort him, he hardly slept and was an extremely difficult eater. As he got older, we could see something wasn't right. He still had no speech, he would sit by himself outside for hours and throw dirt up in the air and watch it falling down. He'd have huge tantrums, dropping himself to the ground screaming, banging his head continuously on the floor.

He'd run into walls head first, scratch, hit, and bite himself. Despite all of this, the doctor would dismiss my concerns, assuring me that all children reach milestones at different stages and Brad was probably going through the 'terrible twos'. I was struggling and wondered what I was doing wrong. I was at my wits' end, unsure what to do. Life was chaotic. We thought things couldn't get any worse, until we started to notice a change in Emily. We watched on helplessly as our happy, friendly, engaging little girl became withdrawn and stopped talking. She gradually lost all her speech and blank distant stares replaced the beautiful sparkle in her eyes. She began odd behaviours, but different from Brad's. She'd line up all her shoes, pencils, toys, and so on, in perfectly straight lines.

She would spin herself around and around in circles. When she'd get excited she'd flap and clutch her hands tightly together, contorting her face and making a humming noise. She had no fear or sense of danger. Once, while out driving, she had unclipped her seat belt and climbed onto the open window. I turned around just in time to stop her from falling out of the car. Brad and Emily would have inconsolable tantrums and were out of control. Taking them out became too much of a stressful battle. I was exhausted and mentally drained.

In 2000, we moved to a larger, coastal town. We enrolled Brad into pre-school, and within a few days of Brad attending, the staff took me aside expressing their grievous concerns about Brad's odd behaviour and slow development. With a joint effort from a psychologist, paediatrician, and pre-school staff, we finally had a diagnosis - autism. A few months later, Emily was also diagnosed. The grief was immense. So began our autism journey.

The paediatrician offered little hope for their future. The feeling of grief and sadness was overwhelming. I asked him 'What do I do?' He handed me a book called *Raising An Autistic Child* and told me to read it. The book was depressing and absolutely no help at all! I began to do some research of my own. Although still stricken with grief, I felt a sense of relief, for at least now it gave me an understanding of my children.

I researched as much information as I could and looked for advice to help manage their challenging behaviours. An awesome psychologist gave me wonderful, invaluable, ongoing advice on how to deal with their self-harm, toileting issues, and destructive behaviour. I went to many autism workshops and seminars, learning how to bring out the best in them. Although both Brad and Emily have autism, they are so very different from one another so sometimes what worked well for Brad would not work for Emily (and vice versa). It was trial and error.

I very quickly learned that having a routine is a major key factor in reducing their anxiety levels and therefore minimising tantrums and meltdowns.

At one of the autism workshops, I learned about 'Reward Chart Systems,' to help establish specific routines/task. Using this system, I decided to set up a 'bedtime routine' reward chart. The task was for Brad and Emily to put on their pyjamas, brush their teeth, and be ready for bed. I used pictures of Elmo from Sesame Street brushing his teeth and putting on his pyjamas to help them follow the steps. If they completed the task, they each got a gold star, placed it on the chart next to their name and got a reward (an inexpensive toy from the $2 store).

I was amazed to see this work so well in such a short space of time! I gradually moved those rewards to once a week and eventually phased the chart out when they were in a solid bedtime routine.

I learned to manage destructive behaviour by remaining calm, ignoring the behaviour, and using distractions to shift their attention. I'd make a huge deal of positive behaviour by giving them lots of praise.

One of the more crucial things I learned was the difference between a tantrum and a meltdown. This gave me such a different perspective and insight on their behaviour. Like every child, they had tantrums out of frustration and tiredness, whereas meltdowns occurred through no fault of their own but rather from a complete loss of control triggered from the complexities of autism. Small changes in routine, being overwhelmed, being hurt or in pain, stress, sensitivity to loud noises, bright lights, large crowds, and even strong odours were just some of the triggers. Severe tantrums could also escalate into a meltdown.

The psychologist was confident that with time they would adapt and learn how to tolerate loud noises, crowds, and so on. He suggested I choose a quiet, less busy time of the day and take them to the local shopping centre, starting with just a few times a week and gradually building up to every day.

I knew this was going to be difficult but I never anticipated the cruelty of people and the hurtful comments. My kids were called everything from rotten spoiled brats to little monsters. At first it was really upsetting, but in the end their comments only made me stronger and even more determined to keep going. I didn't have the energy to deal with their ignorance; I simply returned their insults with a big smile. My kids were making great progress, that's all that mattered.

Brad was almost five years old and was still using nappies, as was Emily. It was time to give toilet training another go. Once again, giving them an incentive worked really well. They each had a special toy they could 'only' play with while they sat on the toilet. I would sit and read them a book—they loved the *Elmo Uses The Potty* book! It's filled with lots of funny pictures and shows Elmo learning to use the toilet. When Brad and Emily did a wee or poo, I used lots of cheering, clapping, and over-the-top praising! It was a slow and tedious process but I'd learnt well enough from past experience that I had to keep going, as stopping only made it even harder to start over again. With patience and persistence, they now use the toilet independently.

We began speech therapy. We changed therapists four times before we found the right one! The therapist gave me loads of games and fun ideas to work on their speech. The fun activities not only helped develop their speech, it also taught them social skills such as waiting for their turn. When they spoke, I encouraged them to face me and make eye contact. These fun activities were bringing us closer together; we were bonding and connecting with one another. Brad's speech came on surprisingly quickly. He went from no speech to non-stop talking! He would continually quote lines from his favourite movies and cleverly use them to express himself. He'd repeat old slang expressions he'd hear from his grandad: it was so funny hearing Brad coming out with things like 'What a pearler', and using it in the right context too!! Emily needed more intense speech therapy. We're still working on her speech, but she now has simple language skills. More importantly, she is happy and smiling again. After years of not hearing her beautiful little voice, the feeling was indescribable the first time I heard her call me mummy.

Brad now began primary school. He had a teacher's aide helping him throughout the day. At times, it was heartbreaking seeing him in the school playground by himself during recess and lunch, but for the most part he was happy being left alone. He needed that time on his own to de-stress from all the pressures and expectations of being in a classroom. As the years went by, he adjusted to school life, his confidence grew and his personality began to show. He would participate in all activities, and he had a group of friends that the teacher's aide described as his entourage! Most of the kids grew to accept and embrace him for who he was.

Emily's pervasive developmental delay and learning difficulties meant she needed specialist support. She was enrolled in a special support unit, dedicated solely for kids with special needs. I was reluctant to place her in the unit, but I knew in my heart there was no way she would cope with mainstream schooling. It proved to be the right decision for her, the high level of care and education she received was absolutely fantastic. Emily started to blossom.

Brad is currently in Year 12. His schoolwork has been modified to suit his level of understanding, and he has a teacher's aide helping him with the subjects he struggles with. He's a computer whiz and has a remarkable memory.

Emily is in Year 10 and in mainstream school with a teacher's aide helping her for the majority of the day. Although Emily's not as high functioning as

Brad, she shines brightly in her own way. She's kind and gentle, very clever, and has an incredible eye for detail.

Unfortunately, both Brad and Emily developed epilepsy during puberty; this is common with autism, and is brought on by teenage hormonal changes.

Thankfully, Brad hasn't had a seizure for quite some time. Emily hasn't been as lucky; she's on the highest dose of medication they give, but she still has seizures. I'm hoping her epilepsy will phase out, as Brad's did. Despite the added challenge of epilepsy, they continue to make dramatic leaps forward. The goal now is to keep building on their strengths, confidence and life skills to further their independence as much as possible. It has been difficult and yes, they still have the impairments of autism, but long gone are the days of self-harm, uncontrollable behaviours and meltdowns. They are lovely, kind-hearted individuals that make the most of each day. Brad and Emily are proof that people with autism do not have any limit to their potential and beyond. I love them dearly and am so very proud of them.

(Left): Brad and Emily. (Right): Robbie and I attended high school together. This is the two of us at Cabramatta High School, NSW, in 1981.

Anonymous

Hi Angelica,

Thanks for your letter.

We wanted to know the *exact* diagnoses for N as well, but in the end someone wisely told us: *Well, it doesn't really matter what his diagnoses is – these are his deficits and this is still the same way to help him, no matter what his label is.*

N's diagnoses of *mild to moderate autism* covered his difficulties in severe speech delay—which included receptive as well as expressive language, nonacceptance of change of routine, social inaction and some repetitive behaviour such as spinning things, rewinding a part of a video and watching it over and over, lining things up, and of course screaming.

We often thought his diagnoses were wrong because he was so clever in a lot of areas, but now we realise sometimes he tricked us! He is a very clever little boy and VERY SMART with computers/Nintendo/and so on. However, he is fantastic at imitating, and we used to assume that he understood everything he was imitating. I vividly remember the cold hand that wrapped around my heart the day I realised that he had absolutely no understanding of what he had just imitated. Then I realised that he had no understanding of *anything* he imitated. He had tricked us *because* he imitated so well.

So I guess that *mild autism* means that Edan has sufficient learning difficulties which meet the criteria for diagnoses of autism, although he must have a number of strengths as well. The features you list from the *Checklist for Autistic Behaviour* that Edan *does not* do are probably a good indication of the behaviour/difficulties of a child diagnosed with moderate to severe autism.

Stop blaming yourself for Edan's difficulties!!! Children with autism don't learn from the everyday environment like their peers. Edan would no doubt have been presented with enough stimuli for learning. However, because of his difficulties he just needed it to be presented to him in a different way. Our home life, school system and society in general teach almost everything using an *auditory* procedure. These kids have VERY POOR auditory skills. That's why, if you change how things are presented to them (N is a great visual learner), then they have a chance of learning.

From your letter, how you write about your son, and what you are doing for Edan, you are a fantastic mum!

Have you connected with an autistic association or a family support group in your area? The latter are a great tool for us. No doctor or association helped us as much as the parent support group did.

I wish you luck and peace Angelica.
5 September 1999.

More ASD reflections by Niko Gambeli

Angelica: Niko, in your 57 years, how did you see ASD diagnoses unfold in the U.S?

HA! Yea, that is pushing it on my knowledge of others. I've never been active with any support groups here in my community. Outside of that, everything from the Facebook community is all hearsay, I'll relate a little farther down. The first formal Asperger's diagnoses (here in the States) was after 1994, when it was recognized by the DSM-IV. I became aware of it somewhere around 1996. Otherwise, for decades, the definition I had of me was 'mild autism'. I was never evaluated in school, never saw a therapist, I was told to deal with the symptoms or to 'stop doing that'. I didn't have the capacity or the tools to comply, so my bedroom became a refuge away from the constant noise and criticism from adults and the taunting from kids. It wasn't until my 30's that I started gaining a little savvy. In fact…that correlated to within a year of my dad's death.

I don't have substantial testimony of my past behaviours from anyone outside of myself—mainly because people didn't put two and two together, or had the attitude of 'everyone does that'. Sure, every Neurotypical does display a bit or two of ASD in one aspect or another. However, Aspies have dozens of attributes, many of them severe enough to affect daily function. Nothing changed in my situation after my awareness or the diagnoses. The only difference was my research and new awareness of the 'hows' and 'whys' of my past, the present, and my possible future.

Resources for adults are extremely limited; most of it goes to children. How ASDs are 'handled' varies. We have one main entity of the USA dictating certain criteria. Fifty different states with fifty different policies and thousands of counties and school districts, and each with something different. Finally, every therapist and every doctor has a different opinion.

In order to receive any help from the state, I'd have to be re-evaluated. There's no one in Colorado qualified to diagnose adults—or, at least, no one advertises that they have the skills. Again, the focus and money is with children. There is something I may be able to relate from other Aspies… many of us born before roughly 1974 feel like a lost generation. Many weren't helped in school, supported at home, and had nowhere to go nor anyone to go to. It depended a lot on the spectrum cards you were dealt as to how you were able to function out there in 'NT land'. Many times, certain symptoms become more pronounced as others retreat; also, some symptoms may get worse with age. None of it is 'cured', just handled to whatever extent we can manage—either well or badly, and at a tremendous expense of physical and mental energy. All these years, I've only known for sure of one other Aspie. But, he dropped out of our social group due to a mountain of physical and mental processes outside of ASD, so I didn't get too much exposure to him.

I will say, from the minute I met this individual, I suspected he was Aspie. Some things raised the flag:

One: His frank expression of things that, by most polite standards, you'd only discuss privately with your doctor. For instance, he piped up with a public and graphic announcement of his reproductive plumbing problems that made all of us in our social support group squirm.

Two: He had no sense of personal space. He had no clue that it was inappropriate to invade someone else's space.

Three — I thought that I, me, myself, had poor Theory of Mind. This guy was way out there. I have rarely come across people so drastically self-centred and unaware, and attributed a lot of his awkwardness to youth and naiveté — he was 28 at the time. Many of us can learn and adapt beyond certain aspects of the spectrum cards — again, that's not a cure.

OTHER'S EDAN

A Facebook Conversation Excerpt About Relationships

Niko

I just completed your chapter on ploughing through different companions. For better or worse, we're conditioned to believe we need people on an emotional basis. It took me a long time to reverse that brainwashing. I really do enjoy being a hermit! Some people can enjoy the people they're with. I don't, or at least, I rarely do. When I am with people, even those I'm familiar with, my stress level goes through the roof. There's just no comfort zone. I have to force myself to get out to support group, to lunch or the pub, or to invite people on hikes (more of a demand of my mom because she's oppressive when I'm out solo). Obviously, we can't go into these relationships gazing into a crystal ball to see how things turn out years from now. Too bad, it would sure save a lot of time, and I'm OCD selfish with my time!

Animals RULE! But, mostly DOGS.

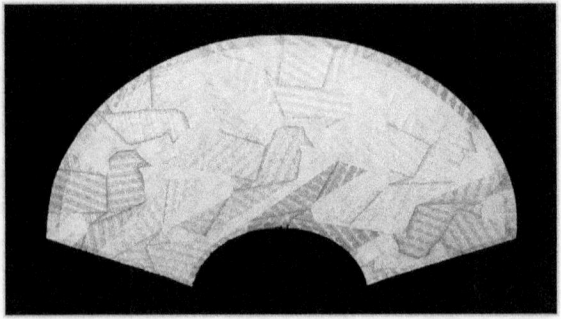

Niko is an accomplished artist whose work is privately sold or in exhibitions. This piece is titled 'Bird and Waterholes' (Mixed media on handmade mica paper 15x30") © Pica2 Graphics

"Dragon Totem"
(Mixed media collage with handmade mica paper 18x24") © Pica2 Graphics

Lee Casuscelli
High School Friend, ASD Advocate and Deputy National Director ASPECT, Autism Spectrum Australia

I would like to begin by noting the significant contribution of people with autism in developing my current understanding of what it means to have autism. I have had the honour and privilege of working with individuals on the spectrum for close to 20 years. Over this period of time, I have been continually surprised by the talents of many, captivated by the skill and knowledge of others and moved by the strength and courage of all. To exist and survive in a world where there is much confusion and misunderstanding is certainly characteristic of those with autism.

My introduction to autism was quite unexpected and perhaps not so well received at first. With little knowledge and no experience, I was like so many others, fast-tracked to the role of chief organiser, decision maker, translator, mediator, social co-ordinator, visual maker, and so much more. Twenty years later, and I was now celebrating this overnight induction to what is still a world of many unanswered questions.

I would say that, although I have learnt a lot since those early years, I believe that I still have a long way to go. Learning is a continuous journey of discovery, and as long as I continue to work with unique individuals, my learning will never be done. As I travel around Australia for work, I am continually humbled by the families living with autism under the most difficult of circumstances. I have confirmed for myself that autism knows no boundaries. It touches lives without warning and, as I write this entry, there are parents all around the world hearing the words for the first time … 'Autism Spectrum Disorder'.

Autism Spectrum Disorder is known as a lifelong developmental disability. It is a complex disability for which there is, as yet, no known cure. As the name implies, autism ranges from mild to severe, and no two individuals are alike. I have yet to meet two individuals that present the same characteristics. I think this area has fuelled my interest, as I continue to learn from each and every individual I meet. I am constantly challenged by the diversity of autism and intrigued by the degree to which these unique characteristics can be supported.

I think I can confidently say I have worked with individuals over the years that span the full range of the spectrum, yet I'm sure I haven't seen it all. I have heard the first words of many children and cheered loudly for many others, but I've also shared the frustrations of too many and the disappointment of more than I can count. I've seen enormous advancements in this field over the years but, as with most things, we still have a way to go.

There is little doubt that we are in an age of evidence. We are actually awash with data, evidence, and theory. There is progress and there is much to celebrate. Autism awareness continues to grow and more and more Australians are today, at least familiar with the term autism and or Asperger's. The veil of silence is lifting and most, if not all, schools across Australia will have at least one association with a child with an Autism Spectrum Disorder. We are talking more about autism, we are sharing more about autism and most importantly, we are celebrating autism.

As I write this entry, we are fast approaching April, the month of celebration for the autism community. As a nation, we stop to acknowledge those with Autism Spectrum Disorders on April 2nd. We even light up the Sydney Opera

House with the characteristic tones of blue to represent autism. These national gestures have significantly lifted the profile of those living with autism and increased public awareness. I like to think that there is less shame and blame, and I continue to commit to the logic that we are all indeed different and unique.

It is the sharing of real stories and the open, honest reflections of those living with and supporting those with autism that are advancing this acceptance. Books such as this that tell it exactly how it is open the eyes and hearts of others. We can study autism for years and devour book after book on the topic, but until we walk in the shoes of those with the condition, we never truly know the reality of the experience.

I met Angelica as a shy, young teenager full of potential. I was in awe of her beautiful voice and impressed by her frank, often misunderstood reflections. We shared a love of English and maybe even a shared crush on the same teacher (we have never discussed this until now). What we didn't share at the time was our experience of autism, so it is only now many, many years later that we have been brought back together through fate. For this I am very grateful.

I commend Angelica and Edan for sharing their story as we can learn much from their journey and hopefully take forward their message of hope.

Lee and Angelica during a visit to Sydney

Edan's Work Reference From Jim And Chris Bowden

To Whom It May Concern,

Re: Edan Galbraith

Edan is sixteen years old and suffers from Asperger's syndrome. He first came to work in the store last year under his school's work experience program. This was one day per week for ten weeks. Edan's work hours were 9am until 3pm with two breaks of twenty minutes each and one hour for lunch. On completion of the work experience, we continued to employ Edan on a casual basis for three hours on Saturday mornings.

Edan's tasks included general cleaning, watering plants, arranging stock on shelves, checking sell-by dates, and assisting customers in the store. He also assisted in the delivery of small items of furniture and domestic gas bottles.

Because of his disability, Edan requires precise instructions. However, once he has been shown exactly what is required, he will work away quietly and diligently until the task is completed.

Neat and tidy in his appearance, Edan is a very polite young man with a quiet demeanour who was invariably punctual. We were sorry to see him leave and would employ him again if he returned to Springton.

JAMES BOWDEN

Springton General Store

10 January 2013

(Left) The Springton General Store. (Right) Edan's precise pencil sketch.

Epilogue Parts One, Two and Three.

Around October 2013, Edan realised his mistake and asked to return to Adelaide to live with Adam and me.

Naturally, I said he could return. I would never deny Edan his maternal home. My door is open to all of my children. The problem for Edan, however, was his father. Something I warned Edan about before he left.

Edan's father and I did not get on. This goes without saying, but my ex-husband loved his children and divorce took them away from him. He would pull out all the stops to get them back. So when he got Edan back, he wasn't going to let go of him again so readily. I am certain there was a lot of emotional manipulation involved here—something Edan is helpless to combat. It was partly this manipulation that took Edan back to Sydney. It's okay. I don't blame my ex-husband. I manipulated Edan enough not to leave.

Becoming a man means learning to make firm decisions, develop assertiveness, and stand up for one's goals and dreams. It was too easy for me to just *take* Edan and fight his father to keep him here. This was Edan's decision and it would have to be *Edan* who fought for it. Edan had to step out of the protected child cocoon and learn about life.

Edan's father had gone to great lengths to accommodate Edan, spending in excess of $40,000 to make the basement of his small house liveable. Edan was enrolled into a horticultural TAFE course. His disability allowance was being saved towards a future investment property for him, and was not spent on general household bills, as I might have.

Additionally, Edan's father tried to 'cure' Edan's Asperger's, much as I did, by placing him on a no carbs, no added preservatives diet he had read about, which proved successful with some ASD children. Edan soon became so terribly thin that his sister Alycia spoke to their father and demanded Edan be taken off the diet immediately.

Yes, Edan's clothes aren't ironed, no one is running around making sure Edan is washing or brushing his teeth each night, and the Risperidone has been thrown out the window, but Edan is loved just as much over there as he is over here, and that is all that matters. Sharing a bunk bed in the 'dungeon room' with her brother isn't ideal for twenty-two-year-old Kristen, but the fact that they are reunited, and that, once again, Kristen resumes a motherly role with Edan, also gives me peace of mind.

Edan's phone calls to us on Friday nights were full of regret. There were uncharacteristic admissions of love and lots of exclamations of 'I miss you' coming from him. My heart leaped with joy hearing them. Then, one Friday, instead of waiting for me to pass the receiver to Adam, Edan requested to speak to him first.

When I saw Adam's face light up and heard my darling husband reply, 'I love you too, Edan!' I knew what was going on. Oh, how I wanted my boy back!

Edan was afraid to speak to his father. He had attempted to explain himself verbally on a few occasions, and his father had offered Edan every reason there was not to leave Sydney. So Edan revisited the only form of communication he had left when talking was just too hard and got you nowhere. He wrote his dad a long letter:

To Dad

Hey Dad,

I've decided that I want to move back to Adelaide to live with my mum again because I find it a lot easier to cope with my problems over there and there's less people living in my mum's house, there's just only my mum and her husband Adam, no kids to annoy me which is just the way I like it.

They at least have one pet cat living with them and that's Mango but Mango is a nice and quiet animal who doesn't bother me and I really miss seeing and playing with Alycia's puppy dog Gogo and Gogo comes to visit a lot at Mum's house which gives me the chance to see her a lot more if I ever still lived with my mum.

I really miss my mum every day because she gets sad very easily for the times when I leave Adelaide when the school holidays finish and my mum also goes through some hard times as well like with work, and there was this one time where my mum left her job being a prison guard because someone was mean to her there, and she cried her head off, but Adam made her feel better but she was crying very heavily for a while and when I was listening to it, it made me almost cry and also feel completely sorry for her, so I want to support my mum whenever she's feeling upset about something that's as bad as losing her job because Mum cares about me a lot as well.

I also want to get to know Adam a lot more as well because when I was living in Adelaide before, me and Adam did a couple of fun activities together but he also worked a lot as well and the times when he stays home on the weekend, he still works a lot, like for when he does some of his stuff in the shed, when he repairs things and when he's busy doing gardening work, so all of that slowed us down with spending time together and I don't see him at all now because I live in Sydney so I feel quite upset about that. And I feel sad for leaving my high school because I had really nice teachers and a lot of friends and I miss my best friend Yanek a lot who I hardly see anymore, and another reason why I want to go back to Adelaide is because I didn't like the sound of what my stepmother said about how there's going to be a lot more people living here.

She said soon her father and mother are both going to be living with us here and she also said that she is thinking of having another baby child, so there will be you, her, Annabella, Kristen, your mother-in-law and father-in-law and that second baby child that my stepmother wants, so there might be seven people that I have to live with. I don't think I could survive even one day listening to two kids screaming all day it would be like a nightmare for me.

You look at it this way, there are seven people living in this house and that's only if you do end up having a second baby girl or boy, and there are only two people living in Mum's house in Adelaide, I would sure rather two than seven. Two people give me more peace; seven is the really noisy one. Plus I really miss having sleepovers with Yanek, I mean I know I can have sleepovers with him during the school holidays, but if I was still living with my mum at Adelaide, I would have a lot more sleep overs with Yanek than I normally do, plus I really enjoyed and miss doing the art class at my high school over there and I'm not so much enjoying the horticulture classes at TAFE. The theory work is very hard and confusing, and I really want to finish Year 11 and 12 at high school back at Adelaide with my friends and all the polite teachers. My art teacher at my high school in Adelaide is just as nice and easy going as my art teacher Norma is over here.

By me wanting to come and live here with you in Sydney, I just wanted to see if it would be any better than living with my mum because I was having a lot of problems before living in Adelaide; it was because of me not handling certain types of noises because of my Asperger's, but when I returned to Adelaide to see my mum on the holidays, I got a lot better and I managed to get over those habits about not liking certain noises and everything was just fine for me over there.

So can I please, please move back to live with my mum because life is just better for me over there, please Dad, I love you!

Love,

Edan xxxxx

Edan in his Harry Potter 'invisibility cloak' and baby Gogo

It was now February 2014, and Edan had made no further progress convincing his dad about returning to Adelaide.

I was going to sadly miss his big eighteenth birthday, but I have promised Edan a trip to the Gold Coast for his nineteenth next year.

For now, Edan seems happy doing a floristry course at TAFE on weekdays and an art course on Saturdays. Adam and I continue to talk to Edan on Fridays, and he keeps up the school holiday visits to Adelaide where he still works for Jim and Chris' Springton General Store of a Saturday morning.

Yanek's and Edan's friendship remains unaffected. They now Skype together and look forward to future sleepovers when Edan is in town.

On a recent visit, Adam and I noticed a regression in the time it takes Edan to do things; namely getting out of the toilet, the bathroom, and preparing for the day's routine. Edan stays up a large portion of the night and wakes up well into the early afternoon hours. He has developed new tics, and still prefers solitary play to integration with family. His verbal communication skills are much better though; Edan now enjoys free flowing and reciprocal conversations with us, which I absolutely love.

I spoke to his father about Risperidone, and it is his opinion that Edan is happy enough without it. Adam and I know that Edan represses his behaviours with his father for fear of reprimand—a fact that has been corroborated by his sister Kristen.

Returning to Adelaide still remains a resolution Edan has to undertake on his own. I make certain I no longer influence him to do differently. At eighteen, Edan is completely free to choose for himself. However, it does become my responsibility to step in if in time I see a distinct emotional deterioration because Edan feels he has no choice.

And I will! Depression and suicidal ideation is common among ASD sufferers. I refuse to lose my Edan to this or any other mitigating circumstance. I love and treasure my boy way too much.

But now it's time to say farewell to sadness, loss, or regret, and bid all an extraordinary

OGWADABWAH-day!

EDAN

Edan is my son

A little angel sent to me,

Or can it be that it is I who chose him?

Or is it me he chose?

People said to me, he is *different*,

That he will never be like others,

I did not believe them,

Edan was simply being himself.

Time passed quickly,

And those people did not change their mind.

Edan has a temper, yes,

But he is not all that different.

I love his caramel eyes,

His tousled auburn hair,

The little freckles on his nose,

His smile and cheeky face.

Had those people been right,

I wouldn't have cared.

Edan is my son,

And I love *him*

Not what people said he *should* be.

Yes, Edan is a very special boy,

He is very special to me.

By Angelica Galbraith, 2001

Edan and me

PART FOUR
The Darker Side

On Valentine's Day 2020, I attended a lecture—quite by accident, mind you—held in the Barossa Valley, only one kilometre from my Friday afternoon job placement, which dealt with managing challenging behaviour in people living with autism (Asperger's syndrome). The subtopics on this material included anxiety, sadness, and anger. The host was a world leading authority on Asperger's syndrome—clinical psychologist, Professor Tony Attwood.

What timing. Just a couple of months ago towards the end of 2019, Adam and I experienced the worst time of our lives with Edan.

Edan Returns From Sydney And His Father's

After almost two years in Sydney living with his father, Edan returns to Adelaide and our new home in Tungkillo, a suburb in the Mid Murray.

Edan cited irreconcilable differences between himself and his father's wife, who was saying things to him which were clearly contrived to get him out of her home. He also deeply hated being sent to TAFE by his father, not understanding theory or the technical side of study at a tertiary level.

Adam and I married in August 2013 and decided to sell my home in Springton and downgrade to a far smaller home we found in Tungkillo, a tiny rural one-horse town situated between Birdwood and Palmer, en route to Murray Bridge. With this 'fait accompli' between his mother and her new husband, Edan had no choice but to acclimatise to this new family setting, or choose life with a non-understanding father and his conspiratorial wife.

I always knew Edan would return one day, so there was a nice modified garage room waiting for him in our new home. What I *hadn't* envisaged though, is that his sister Kristen would also return and reclaim her position living amongst us. Had I foreseen this, I would have clung to the two-story, five-bedroom Springton home.

Because Kristen moved into the modified garage, we were forced to find a small caravan for Edan to live in out in the front yard. In hindsight, given Edan's continuing (though greatly diminished) OCD behaviours, keeping him separate from the core household was a good idea.

Over the next four years, we all got on relatively well. Edan was placed back on Risperidone which appeared to control his mood swings and OCD manias to a large degree. He obtained work as a supported employee with a disability service provider in the Barossa Valley packaging wine and Maggie Beer produce, and the only times Adam and I had any real issues with Edan was when Kristen went that little too far with her sisterly teasing and Edan gave her a few hits to the head with a closed fist for good measure. This, and Adam's face. Edan, who is literal about absolutely everything, could not appear to understand that Adam's furrow was a permanent fixture of his physiognomy and not an expression of his feelings, which Edan translated as unfavourable towards him. Edan once stated Adam looked like actor Steven Seagal, and this comparison may provide an understanding of the appearance of Adam's perceived 'accusatory furrow'.

Kristen, who had lived with Edan in Sydney for a while before his return, concurred that their stepmother's behaviour towards Edan was sometimes quite inflammatory—and although Kristen tended to get on well with her generally, her level of maturity was questionable and a factor which, combined with her father's stubbornness, forced my daughter to leave Sydney.

Asking Kristen what Edan's worst behaviours were whilst at his father's, Kristen reported that Edan once drew a knife from the kitchen cupboard with which he then threatened their father if he didn't allow him to return to us in Adelaide. Edan himself told me he had played truant from TAFE on various occasions because he despaired over his lessons. He'd spend literally the entire day in the college's oval, absently loitering till home time. Once the police accosted him, asking him who he was and what he was doing there. This had frightened him terribly, because police presence signified a threat for him. He had watched many films with his father that were rarely law-enforcement friendly.

The Mirror Cracks

As Edan grew, both in stature and girth, going from the lanky, almost skeletal prepubescent boy I sent away in early 2013, to a young man on the doorstep of his twenty-first birthday, I noticed Edan's emotional and intellectual demeanour change also.

Edan spent a lot of his time playing his video games, as he always had; and his favourite series, The Walking Dead—introduced to us all by Kristen—became his special interest. Edan even attended a 'Walking Dead Sydney' convention in 2018 with Kristen, as chaperone, where he met and posed with one of his favourite characters, 'Simon', played by Canadian actor, Steven Ogg.

Edan posing proudly with Canadian actor Steven Ogg
The Walking Dead convention, Sydney NSW, February 2018

"You know, Mum," Edan informed me excitedly (or as excited as an Aspie gets) "Steven Ogg is Trevor in GTA too!"

What the hell is GTA I thought?

Grand Theft Auto, a series of violent video games which allow the player to become a 'baddy' who wins over the 'goodies' and the police. One guess who had introduced Edan to GTA… no, not Kristen: his father.

Around this time, our little house in Tungkillo was inundated with water during a five-minute flash flood in the region. The fallout from this was momentous for me emotionally due to difficult dealings with our insurance company, where we had to vacate the premises for two weeks and place all of or possessions into a POD out the front of our home.

As I am not always a lateral problem solver, and fearing another devastating event (although my husband fixed the problem by drilling spitters into the eaves), I insisted on moving. I found a beautiful old house in Flaxman Valley, nestled inside a working vineyard. I was once again a Barossa Valley resident.

Edan loved his long solitary walks overlooking broad pastures in rural Tungkillo, often taking these until dusk to get away from Kristen's petty torments, and the persistent coughing of the guy living next door, which was impertinently audible from within his little caravan. There was no doubt in my mind the solitude of the vineyard, with five acres of our own, off the beaten track, and without neighbours, would be manna from heaven for Edan. The house had an annexe too, which once again allowed Edan to be independent from us. He had his 84" TV and every game console known to man inside his Walking Dead 'Woodbury' den, the perfect life for an Aspie bachelor who under no circumstance wished to have a girlfriend or get married—ever!

Edan's beautiful home in Flaxman Valley before he was placed in supported independent living for his and his family's benefit.

As the months at Flaxman Valley flew by, Edan started to exhibit some issues at work. One of his best friends and workmate, Paul, had left with his family for sunnier pastures in Cairns, and Edan began to find his colleague's random sniffs, coughs, perceived jibes at one another and particularly, the radio blaring in the background, increasingly annoying.

Sniffing, coughing, and Edan's perception of 'loud breathing' had always been an issue that appeared to have been lessened by the Risperidone. I remember once driving along the windier portion of the Springton to Williamstown route with Edan completely losing it over my sniffing (I suffer from rhinitis), and then blocking my vision with his hand as he attempted to cup my nose over with such ferocity and anger, I thought we'd hit a tree on the next bend for certain.

"STOOOOOOOP!!!!" Edan screeched furiously, "STOP SNIFFING! And, you're breathing too loud too!"

I proceeded to explain to Edan why I couldn't help both issues; with breathing, I was certain it was actually his own breathing Edan was listening to. I knew Edan understood intellectually and emotionally, but his OCD just could not cope with any of it. Eventually the 'loud breathing' was also being attributed to Adam, and even our dogs Conan and Frodo. But the loudest breather of all was Edan's father.

Alycia took part in Channel 9's social experiment, "Married At First Sight" in September of 2017. Edan was at the filming of her 'wedding' in Melbourne, which was a long, drawn-out affair. Edan sat behind his father during the ceremony, when all of a sudden, between takes, Edan hit himself on the side of the head. Since earlier that year, Edan had started to do this more frequently in order to deal with frustration.

"I fucking can't stand Dad's loud breathing!" Edan spat, almost in tears of frustration.

I readily jumped out of my front row seat and moved Edan towards the back row where my estranged cousins sat, and asked the youngest, who was at that time still the most reasonable to speak with, if Edan could sit next to him, which he did. The filming and fake ceremony/reception continued without another hitch and Edan even managed to score equal billing on the show when Alycia introduced Edan to her new 'husband'.

Towards the end of 2018, Edan's OCD fuelled rages began to rear their awful heads routinely and systematically.

Dr Jekyll And Mr Hyde

Remember the nursery rhyme by Henry Wadsworth Longfellow about the little girl with the little curl right in the middle of her forehead? When she was good, she was very good, but when she was bad she was horrid. Edan soon became synonymous with this ditty.

If you spoke to any of Edan's life/work stakeholders, they would all sing you the same song; *'Why, Edan is such a polite, helpful, and pleasant young man'*.

And indeed Edan *is* such an entity. Added to the above traits, Edan has enormous capability for love and empathy, classing both family and friends as the most important things in his life.

I once had a client who was Asperger's, OCD, and body dysmorphic. He was also psychopathic—a genuine ticking bomb waiting to explode. I had warned the organisation I worked for that I'd seen some traits of sociopathy like the one this client displayed in a couple of criminally challenged charges I had in juvenile detention back in Sydney, but I was only slandered as incompetent for my efforts. Approximately a year later, long after I refused to continue working with this young man (he was seventeen when I first met him and almost nineteen when I left him), his threats of harm to staff became a reality when he attempted to stab a male carer. As much as I absolutely concede that people with Asperger's/autism can have pronounced narcissist traits, and Edan is no different in many of his own attitudes, individuals living with Asperger's and autism are not sociopathic or psychopathic by nature any more than any neurotypical is born with these proclivities. But many Aspies *are* prone to violent behaviour, and Edan's propensity for violence and the ability to hurt others and himself (but mainly himself), was growing at an alarming rate.

Just before Christmas 2017 was when Edan seriously crossed the line, lunging at me, and punched me in the arm and back. I noticed more and more that Edan was not tolerating being reprimanded, or me engaging in the previously comedic yet well-intentioned put downs we threw at one another. Edan was increasingly growing 'offended' by so many everyday occurrences that we were never fully certain what we could say in order not to bring forth a rage attack.

Letter Written To Edan's New Psychologist (27/12/20):

Hi K,

I hope you had a wonderful Christmas and look forward to a wonderful 2019. I know I am!

I have a problem... a BIG one!

So you may recall me telling you my son has Asperger's? In the past few months, his OCDs and general behaviour have escalated, with Edan finding it more and more difficult to manage his reactive aggression towards directives and criticisms whether productive or not. He has had epic meltdowns at work, and last Friday, for the very first time ever, he physically assaulted me and his stepfather. In the past it was verbal assaults, although he has hit his older sister twice.

Edan is very self-aware and understands his explosive behaviour is completely off tap and inappropriate. He apologises soon after he has calmed down and promises to control himself in the future, however we now recognise he has NO impulse control whatsoever and the only thing that 'works' is to interact with him minimally. This is not how we wish to live our lives with my son who also lives with us. We are at the point now where we need to seriously consider police intervention if this reoccurs. Edan is 22.

Edan's current psychologist is in semi-retirement. Her name is Chris B, and she only practices once a month in Birdwood on a Wednesday. Not only is Wednesday a bad day to take Edan to her as we all work, and this means taking a half day's leave to transport him, but I also feel Edan has gone as far as he can go with Chris. All Chris recommends is self-guided meditation (she did this with me also before I began seeing you). Someone like Edan simply cannot reach the intellectual principles and commitment required to achieve and maintain this practice.

I feel Edan is now in dire need of a psychiatrist or a psychologist such as yourself who can apply biofeedback and neurotherapeutic self-regulating methods. Can you help?

I also wish to have Edan change GP in order to get a new pair of ears onto his medication requirements. In the past, his doctor has worked near miracles with Edan in terms of medication (Risperidone), but my mother's intuition is now telling me that based on a new psychotherapist's evaluation of Edan's issues, a medication review is required. The levels of paranoia Edan is now experiencing almost qualify him for an anti-psychotic medication such as Abilify.

Anyway, please get back to me as soon as possible. His next psyche session is on February 6th, and next GP appointment is 15/1, both dates I'd like to avoid so I can start him with new advocates. Do you have any ideas re: a good Barossa GP as well? Preferably one who has a deeper understanding and experience with ASD?

Much obliged to you,

Angelica Brewer

On that pre-Christmas date, Edan was about to go to his Christmas dinner for the general store in which he had worked fortnightly ever since he left school in Year 10. As a 'foodophile', this dinner was an epic event where Edan could literally stuff his face at his boss' expense. He wasn't going to miss it no matter how upset he was.

Yet, upset he was indeed, and he took several breaks from the event to go outside and further abuse me via text. Edan blamed me for ruining his night, and Adam for tackling him away from me. There was no reasoning with him. Edan had to have the last word and boy, could he hold a grudge. Finally, two or so days after this incident, Edan apologised for hitting me and stated he understood why Adam pulled him away from me. Edan, however, insisted I had been the antagonist and not the other way around.

A major narcissistic trait that defines Edan's outbursts is the fact he has to have the last word. If he receives a rebuttal—and particularly from family members (he mostly suppresses with strangers)—he'll continue until the adversary gives up or when Edan, not to be defeated, goes into a major meltdown and forces the issue.

Following this episode, bit by bit, Edan's aggressive streak increased steadily and with it, his OCD behaviours. There were more breaks being taken at work to accommodate his fixation with certain noises and numbers, and semblances of life with Edan before he left for Sydney were returning to haunt us. I noticed I was slowly but surely adapting the way I spoke, and even the way I breathed, in order not to disturb or aggravate Edan. Going to public places like the movies where people would periodically sniff, cough, talk, or sneeze, was becoming exceedingly precarious. Often, I'd wish I could spin the cone of silence over

Edan in order to avoid public meltdowns where I'd feel hopeless, even with all of my prison work conflict resolution experience.

Eventually, it started to become evident what was bothering Edan, as he began to recall and recount portions of his elementary school life I was completely unaware of. Edan had been bullied in primary school in Sydney and PTSD-like flashbacks were instigating some of his rages. Was it possible Edan was becoming a man and rationalising aspects of his past, present, and future? We were told years ago that the emotional intelligence factor in people living with Asperger's syndrome took around seven years to catch up to the person's chronological age, so in essence Edan was twenty-two but still fifteen emotionally.

Despite the awful emotional episodes emerging from my son, glimpses of the sensitive, kind, polite, and sometimes altruistic Dr Jekyll remained. As an amateur astrologist, I couldn't help blame the mutable duality of his zodiac sign of Pisces. But this is where I'll stop attempting to explain things from a mother's lay perspective.

Worth mentioning is the fact that Kristen was now relocating to England in order to pursue new horizons and perhaps a budding online romance as well. En route to Portsmouth, Edan accompanied Kristen in March 2019 for breast enhancement surgery in Thailand. Edan had a minor meltdown when, unassisted by the airline he flew with, he could not be understood exiting customs. Then, in June, he was dealt a second blow when his best friend at work, Paul (who was almost fifty years old), relocated to Cairns in Queensland.

Below is my account of a self-harm and OCD mania episode I found in my documents from the second half of 2016, while we were still in Tungkillo and Edan lived in the caravan.

Edan came into the house at 12pm. He has been sleeping in really late lately. He was having an attack of OCD trying to lock his caravan door. I called Edan inside for lunch several times. He continued with his set of eight counts whilst trying to lock his caravan door.

When he finally came inside, I asked him to eat. He sat down but picked up his serviette, tore it angrily into pieces, and then hit himself in the head. I asked Edan if he needed his valium, he began moaning saying, 'quick give me the fricking tablet!' Edan snatched it off me and roughly swallowed it down with his coffee spilling it all over his muffin. This made him angrier, and he hit himself in the head, began to cry (something he rarely does) and shot up from his seat, announcing that he needed to get out of the house or he would hurt someone. He then asked if he could eat his muffin outside. I said yes, and put him on the back patio to eat. I watched Edan from the kitchen window. He was spilling his coffee everywhere again and shaking. He then hit the side of his head at least 8-12 times as hard as he could. I ran outside and restrained him, taking the cup away as well as his plate. Edan stated the neighbour was talking and he could not stand it. He then stated, 'I fucking hate the number SIX, I could fucking kill it the fucking thing! I can't stand it anymore. I want to kill myself. Right now I need to hurt myself or someone really bad!' Edan added that he thinks he is possessed by the devil and that Kristen told him the devil's number is 666. I attempted to calm Edan down by telling him there is no devil and that some idiot made all of that and '666' up. This calmed him somewhat. I also hugged Edan and he managed to finish his lunch. Edan broke down in tears again.

I told Edan to take a long walk in order to re-group, which he did. After half an hour I drove to the place Edan normally likes to spend time in, approximately two kilometres from home. Edan was there. Edan stated he felt better now he was away from all the noise and talking. He said en route he still had OCD attacks and that he punched a road sign and kicked some stones, but the feeling for hurting himself or others had passed for now. I left Edan and returned home to inform my husband he was temporarily okay.

I informed Edan he may need to be admitted into hospital for some quiet time, and he agreed. He stated he could not stand the noises coming from the TV and the radio, or from us if we said SIX, SICK, ILL, UNWELL or any other related words.

D-Day

As Edan's OCD behaviours increased at an alarming rate, and 'breaks' and minor meltdowns at/from work were becoming more frequent, I sought the opinion of a new doctor who then referred me to an area psychiatrist for a complete review of Edan's medication regime.

Around this time, Edan was also displaying some concerning behavioural changes that appeared to involve his preoccupation with YouTube and his The Walking Dead and Grand Theft Auto video games. I then discovered (by Edan's own admission) that he was dressing up as a character in one of said games, and taking off in the night time after Adam had gone to bed and I was at work overnight, attempting to frighten motorists coming up the rather solitary Eden Valley Road with a fake sword which was a replica in one of his not so confronting video games, but could still cause harm. The walk from our home to this point is a five-kilometre trek utilising a very dark and solitary dirt track. I was beyond terrified at the prospect of Edan engaging in extreme scare tactics of this nature—not just for the sake of public safety, but because I feared the worst case scenario for Edan too. I begged him to never do it again.

When I tried to put on my youth worker and disability support worker hats on and attempted to elicit a reason why Edan was acting out this way, I realised that Edan was now, at long last, trying to make sense of the world around him. Edan first displayed a small portion of his humanitarian concerns when he asked me why Dr Phil (McGraw) was so hard on people coming on to his show for help. I am a Dr Phil aficionado and would catch his program every chance I had, and sometimes Edan would watch it with me. My explanations did not help Edan: if anything they inflamed his awkward sense of justice all the more.

Married at First Sight's scene-stealing brother

Alycia introduces Eden to new husband Mat. Image: Nine Network

(Left) When Edan's oldest sister to part in the Channel 9 production of 'Married at First Sight' in 2018 (Season 5), Edan managed to have his story told on national television. (Top Right) Edan has travelled abroad often with his sisters and father's second family. (Bottom Right) With his middle sister, Kristen, in Thailand.

Then, one night, Edan presented me with a smashed iPhone. I was in shock. Edan's face was crimson red. He tried to explain he was 'sick of the bad guy getting bullied', and that 'even bad guys deserve empathy, and especially from people like Dr Phil and the police, because they're supposed to be helpers'. As a former corrections officer I explained to Edan why sometimes the perpetrator needs a tougher approach but this made no sense to him. His mind was set and he again drew from PTSD-type triggers from his own past, which no doubt were added to by the fact his parents were merciless with one another during their marriage.

Edan was actively seeking out YouTube videos depicting alleged police violence and juvenile delinquency on Dr Phil episodes, among other things. The feelings these raised in him were then exacerbated and compounded by the violence he came across playing GTA and The Walking Dead. In The Walking Dead, Edan felt sorry for the cannibal antagonists, seeking their justification and redemption from situations he would then attribute to himself.

I did not replace the iPhone. Edan used it at work and at bowling on Thursday afternoons (straight after work) to listen to music his sister had downloaded for him, as this was vital in order to drown out some of the OCD behaviours the blaring factory radio was producing, but I had to minimise his exposure to YouTube, so we gave Edan an iPod for work instead.

Angry outbursts with definitive delusional undertones increased from monthly, to weekly, to almost daily. The area psychiatrist prescribed Sodium Valproate for the volatile mood swings and Paroxetine for the OCD behaviours. I then looked into a little known medical practice accredited by my long-term chiropractor called 'The Tomatis Method'. Although the method was developed namely with assisting patients suffering partial hearing impairment, it appeared successful in autistic patients where the re-wiring of brain patterns via auditory pathways helped change perception and triggers. Anything and everything was worth a go in my opinion. I was now so, so scared.

Late July 2019 became D-Day.

(Left) Edan and his best friend at his former work, Paul Humphries, who later relocated to Queensland. (Right) Only days before Edan's complete meltdown. Innocence at its best. Even Caesar (our cat) didn't see what was coming.

That fateful Saturday morning I knew better than to honour Edan's sleepover date with Yanek. Edan looked wild and completely off tap. I woke him up and waited inside until he was dressed and ready to have his breakfast. I must have locked the back entrance door for some reason, and all of a sudden I heard, 'Open this fucking door!' in what can only be described as a voice that was not benign in any way.

Surprised and baffled, I approached the back door and could see the madness in Edan's face. His eyes seem darker than usual, his skin was pasty, and a dark cloud shrouded his entire being. 'Open this fucking door!' he yelled once more. He wasn't joking. We are a family who swears (except for Alycia), so swearing rarely takes me aback, even when it comes from Edan. Edan swore sparingly, though, and usually either in raconteur context or when he'd have a meltdown.

I asked Edan why he swore at me and in the same ominous voice bearing the same shark-like countenance, he replied, 'Because no one shuts me out of my fucking house!'

Edan had attempted to explain something just wasn't right with him on a number of occasions. He told me he often felt like he was going mad. Once, after a fairly intense meltdown where I had to collect Edan early from work, he asked me if he had been a mistake, and whether his life held any value. He began querying my own personal spiritual faith, asking me about the rewards of going to heaven, and not long after our talks on the subject, Edan began the same rebellious God-blaming I heard my mother carry on with many years before, when I was her child living in the narcissistic chaos that was her home. Even the way Edan self-harmed reminded me of my mother. He'd bite his forearms and hands, hit his head, scratch at his face, and curse and scream almost exactly as she did.

I asked Edan if he still wanted to see Yanek. The sleepover had been organised months before and I felt Yanek would somehow pacify or console Edan with whatever it was he was going through. Edan insisted he wanted to see his friend, although he did not feel quite right. I wanted Edan to reassure me he would not hurt anyone or upset Yanek's household, and even though it was said haphazardly, Edan stated he wouldn't.

As we left our driveway Edan burst out with some shocking news.

"I broke the neighbour's window with my sword!"

I couldn't or wouldn't believe what I was hearing.

"I dressed up again last night and threatened cars on the main road, and this man stopped and egged me on, calling me a wimp and a loser, and I tried to hit his car with my sword, but he drove away, and I was so angry and had to have my satisfaction, so I smashed the neighbour's window with the sword. I think my sword is broken too."

I immediately thought Edan had broken the window of a newly renovated chapel that was purchased by a family as their weekender, just under a kilometre down the road from our place. Ironically, the head of this family was in fact a glazier. I shrieked, but Edan corrected me, saying, "No not the church, the winery next door!" My heart skipped a beat. I turned the car around to take a look. We had purchased the house and three adjacent acres from a five star Barossa Valley winemaker, with their VIP tasting rooms located right next door. This, too, had been recently renovated, and yes, the four-panel window was completely smashed.

I held my breath, unable to process what I'd just seen, how I felt about it, how I'd respond to Edan, and what to do next. I knew I had to return home and not go to Yanek's, but right then, right that very moment, I was terrified of my son. I simply did not wish to exacerbate or elevate any other destructive behaviour while on my own with him.

I drove to Williamstown holding my breath and darting frequent glances over to Edan. The dark cloud, the shark eyes, the ominous countenance were all still there. We finally arrived at Yanek's home.

As Edan was greeting his best friend, I spoke to Yanek's parents.

"I'm sorry, but Edan is far from well. He won't be staying the night. He probably should not be staying at all but maybe seeing Yanek will help him?"

I then described to them what transpired, nervously looking over my shoulder to see if Edan was listening or translating my body language. Aspies are very intuitive.

It soon became obvious Yanek's parents, Mel and Chad, were more than a little worried about Edan being in their home. Edan had once put a hole in their brand new house when he suffered a Turophobia spell, fainted, and knocked out some of the gyprock. But today was a far different issue—far different and much worse.

Chad took the boys to the local pub for a meal. Edan loved his food and appeared compliant, but the countenance had not left him. I didn't know what to do. Normally I'd go home and enjoy some Edan-free time. Being the parent of an Aspie isn't usually an easy task. I decided to hang around and debrief with Mel. Chad returned, stating that things appeared to be okay when he'd left. Then the dreaded call arrived. Yanek told Chad he'd better get back to the pub straight away. Edan was going off.

I jumped into Chad's SUV, almost out of my mind with worry and dread. I expected the worst. We arrived at the pub and Edan was seething. Instead of getting into the SUV as instructed, Edan began screaming and swearing. He hurled a can of coke he was drinking out into the neighbouring car park and then ran off onto the road like a bat out of hell, completely out of his mind. I left Chad and Yanek where they were, ordering them to go home and call the police and ambulance. There was no way Edan would be returning home in that state of mind. Yanek reminded Edan they had paid for and ordered their meal, poor bloke.

As I attempted to keep up with Edan, who was now ferociously yelling at passing cars and anyone who was looking, even taking on a dog barking from behind a fence, I texted Mel frantically, inquiring about an estimated time of arrival for either the police or ambulance. I managed to steer Edan into a churchyard, where I had him do laps around the property and away from people's homes. My juvenile justice training kicked back in and I kept Edan talking about any other subject than why he was so enraged. Anger was simply a by-product of a much greater complexity no one, not even Edan, could figure out—at least not at this very moment in time. As I kept talking to Edan, I continued texting Mel. Then Chad arrived. I gestured for him to keep a good distance away from us. He held a phone to his ear so I knew he was in contact with the authorities. I just had to continue to keep Edan away from others, talking, walking, and getting tired so that the peak of his stress and anxiety would eventually taper off and subside.

It was at least forty-five minutes of performing this ritual when the Nuriootpa police finally arrived. I had also begged Adam to leave work and come to the scene from the Adelaide Remand Centre in the city. By now, Edan had managed to calm down somewhat and took a seat on the floor, resting against the cold stone of the church wall. The police officers on the scene approached Edan, speaking to him in the gentlest of voices. Although Edan originally stated to me that if I called the 'fucking cops' he'd assault them cos he 'wasn't fucking going to gaol!' he respectfully greeted them and answered all of their questions. Two more police arrived from Gawler Police Station, then Adam, and finally the ambulance. Edan quickly rose up from the spot he'd occupied for almost half an hour and ran to Adam, hugging him tightly as he begged for forgiveness. I was an absolute mess of emotions.

Edan was then transported to the Lyle McEwan Hospital's emergency department as Adam and I followed. I thanked Chad and Mel (who arrived later to offer assistance) and inquired whether Yanek was okay. Yanek had been very brave but also heartbroken in witnessing his best friend's downward spiral. The negative side of Asperger's syndrome affects everyone.

I called the vineyard's owner and explained his broken window. This winemaker was among the few five star winemakers in the region, and I felt embarrassed and afraid of his reaction, but he was extremely understanding. I assured him the window would be fixed and paid for as soon as possible.

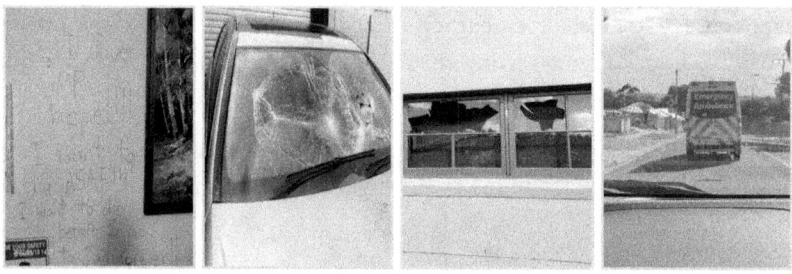

(Left) Edan took up the habit of defacing walls with pleas, which at times bordered on the obscene and obscure. (Left middle) A carer's car smashed because of a verbal trigger unbeknownst to the carer (Right middle) Edan smashed the winery next door to our home in Flaxman Valley with his fake Zelda Sword (Right) Following the ambulance carrying my precious son. I never believed a day like this could ever arrive.

Diagnostics

After two harrowing days in the emergency department, Edan was transferred to the mental health assessment unit of the Lyle McEwan Hospital.

Edan remained there for just over a week. He was compliant and settled, and following a brief conference with his duty doctor, which Edan's father also attended, it was determined that Edan could return home without a change of medication, something I had asked the hospital to review.

We resumed his disrupted Tomatis therapy, although I was certain it wasn't actually helping him… maybe even disrupting things further. I had to continue trying everything I could, though. At this point in his and our lives, EVERYTHING was worth a try, and boy had I tried *everything* since Edan was first diagnosed at age three, even when I thought his doctors may have gotten things wrong.

Edan returned to work after a rigorous return-to-work conference held with his managers, where a management plan was drawn up to meet with Edan's new emotional requirements. Only a week after, I received a call from his direct overseer informing me Edan had had words with another supported employee and ran out of work with his bag 'like a bat out of hell', nowhere to be found, even when a supervisor got straight into the car to look for him.

I must have called Edan two dozen times on his phone (a new one his sister in England had sent him) over the course of that day without any answer. I then decided to resist setting out in the car to look for him. I was beginning to feel more frustration with Edan than fear for his welfare. Maybe what Edan needed was a lesson rather than empathetic rescuing? But by five in the afternoon, almost five hours after receiving the alert call from his work place, I thought I should look for him.

I drove just one and a half kilometres from my home and saw Edan on the side of the dirt road. He looked positively dejected. He had just walked *twenty-nine kilometres!*

"Why, Edan, why?" I asked him when he got into my car, exhausted and positively miserable.

"Robert at work told me he earned more than me, and I felt heartbroken and just had to get out of there before I picked up a wrench and was going to hit him on the head with it."

When we arrived home, Edan fell onto the driveway and could not move. He had been wearing his steel capped boots and his feet looked like hell.

I, in turn, had fallen into hell. What was I to do now?

The following week Edan was back in the Mental Health Assessment Unit. He had hurt himself so badly by smashing his head onto our gravel road, I called his father at nine o'clock that night to take him to the emergency department himself, simply because Adam and I couldn't cope anymore and I knew calling the police would be of little use whilst Edan was safely away from the public on our property.

Only the day before, I couldn't find Edan anywhere around the property. Fearing the worst, I drove the four kilometres to Eden Valley Road, and sure enough, there he was returning from the main road carrying Adam's baseball bat and wearing The Walking Dead's 'The Governor' character's brown vest. Edan had gone out attempting to frighten vehicles driving by.

I had already confiscated all of his GTA and The Walking Dead video games, stopped Edan from watching Season Nine of The Walking Dead series, taken his Zelda shield and what was left of Link's sword after he smashed the window, along with his Harry Potter cape, and now The Governor's vest and eye patch. All of Adam's sporting bats were secured, and the keys to Adam's gun safe were relocated, as Edan had mentioned arming himself with these at some point. Shit just got real.

Edan was now saying terrible things like, 'I want to kill babies and murder an innocent person' in the throes of a rage fuelled meltdown. The self-harming intensified. Sometimes Edan resembled the stereotypical demonically possessed individual of films similar to *The Exorcism of Emily Rose*. What had happened to my son?

After a second fruitless discharge from the Mental Health Assessment Unit where his medication *was* reviewed by the hospital's duty psychiatrist, Edan's employers were less generous and trustworthy with his behaviour management plan. Edan could only return to work half a day once a week for a month.

Edan during visiting hours in the mental health assessment unit. A very comfortable, patient friendly place that did nothing to alter Edan's precarious, unpredictable, and downright dangerous situation.

In October 2019, while Adam and I travelled to Sydney for a friend's wedding, Edan remained at his father's house with his stepmother and eight-year-old half-sister. The new doses of Sodium Valproate appeared to have subdued the frequency and intensity of his rages, and although still highly worried and sceptical, Adam and I felt that a change of environment and the presence of Edan's father should mean that, at worst, Edan would suppress his feelings of antagonism, or at best, cruise through the next four days enjoying himself.

On our drive back to my ex-husband's house to collect Edan and get back home after the four days away, I received a frantic call from his new wife stating that Edan had had a meltdown at the dinner table and run outside somewhere into the community, screaming, cursing, and stating he was going to kill his father and anyone else who crossed his path. Adam wanted to drive there faster, but couldn't. South Australia is a nanny state. I texted Edan's stepmother asking her what sparked the meltdown. She texted back about Edan's father and Edan having a conversation about God.

Because of my spirituality and what Edan had learned at school, Edan was formulating his own interpretation of God and parochial justice. The take on God that Edan's father was pushing on this day was the eternal 'bad versus evil' debate, which was something Edan could not engage in due to his current state of mind. I was almost certain I had made this clear before we left.

We finally pulled into the driveway. Edan's stepmother and and little sister stood there huddled together, visibly shaken. Edan's stepmother informed us that Edan had run off to the nearby reserve and his father was there with him now. I could see father and son in the distance. It was an odd scene, as his father was shirtless and was attempting to straighten himself out. Edan was followed by that damned dark cloud, I could see as much. I yelled out to him from my vantage point; "How are you, Edan?"

"Not good," came his reply.

As Edan and his father drew closer, I received the full picture of what had obviously transpired between the two of them. They both sported bloodied faces and their clothes were covered in dirt. One or the other had crossed the line into serious physical assault. Oh my God… I quickly gestured to Edan's stepmother to go inside with her child.

Edan's father trailed a few steps behind when Edan suddenly turned around, ran at his father, and dropped three punches into his head. His father was trying to defend himself from the blows, imploring Edan to stop, saying that he didn't wish to fight any longer. I cried out for Edan to stop and Adam was quick to tackle Edan and pull him off his father. It was a pitiful sight to witness.

I asked Edan's father if he wanted to press charges. At this point in Edan's illness, police involvement on a punitive level could be just what Edan needed, Asperger's syndrome or not. This was a serious criminal act that required serious dealing with. His father stated he did not wish to press charges and then quickly went into his house. Adam and I could not leave the scene with Edan on board fast enough. I again did my best to talk Edan down, as his heightened state compelled him to stick his finger up at other motorists and yell out threats and curses to passers-by. Adam rapidly activated the window lock mechanism and took Edan home to wash off the horror of what he had done to his own father.

According to Edan, he had simply wished to remove himself from the discussion after his father ignored his wanting to stop talking about the subject of retribution, and when his father continued, Edan lost his temper, told him and his sister to *fuck off* (later repenting about his sister) and stormed off to cool down at the reserve. Instead of respecting Edan's wishes and waiting it out, his father followed Edan to the reserve and, when he apparently heard Edan curse at a mother and her child there, he decided to redirect Edan's ire towards himself by asking Edan if he wanted to fight him. This then is when Edan threw the first punch, which was subsequently reciprocated by his father.

I had thought Edan hitting me had crossed a serious line, but what he did to his father was far worse.

Food soothes the savage beast: Edan's facial injuries just the day after his altercation with B. B definitely came out of it second best with several lacerations on his face.

Edan's psychologist was extremely angry that Edan had been placed in such a position, given his diagnosis and what was now happening for him. My ex-husband and I had a long history of violent confrontations throughout our marriage, and although I am in no way taking away from Edan's culpability in this matter, to goad someone in such a position as Edan's is irresponsible and short-sighted, and I was angry with my ex-husband and told him so.

This horrible incident took away our only days of continuous, much-needed respite. Understandably, Edan's father and his family did not wish to see Edan again for a very long time, and this feeling was reciprocated by Edan himself, his psychologist, me, and Adam. Edan was angry that his dad asked him to fight him, leaving Edan without a choice not to, because as we all knew only too well, Edan *had* to have the last say and final triumph at all costs. Still, I understood how his father might have thought he was saving the stranger in the reserve and her child.

By the time Adam and I arrived home with Edan, he had settled down considerably. Adam attended to his wounds, and we gave Edan a full Quetiapine tablet to get him to sleep off what other residual angst might still be boiling deep inside of him. These had been prescribed on a needs-only basis by the Mental Health Assessment Unit duty doctor. Adam suspected a fractured nose, but fortunately it was a false alarm.

Selfishly, I allowed Edan to attend work, because I needed things to be as normal for him and us as possible. He explained to his colleagues his dad accidentally hit him in the face with a football, whilst I explained a part truth to his supervisors. At the end of the day, Edan was a major risk to himself and others, and he should not have returned to work until we could sort out what was happening for him.

Hindsight is 20/20, alas, and on the sixth of December, Edan committed the unimaginable.

Autistic Terrorism

On the way to work, everything appeared okay. Edan liked to lie back in his seat listening to CD's playing while I tickled his hand with my non-steering one. When we had almost reached his work, my chiropractor and Tomatis practitioner called and, unfortunately, her message went through the speakers so that Edan was privy to our conversation. I shouldn't have taken the call. Damn you, 20/20 hindsight!

The practitioner was concerned that because of Edan's present emotional condition, her highly expensive equipment might be in danger. The practitioner then directed the call at Edan and Edan, feeling he was being reprimanded, lost it, and began hitting himself viciously.

I should have turned right around and taken him home but I didn't, again alas, due to selfishness on my part. I had Edan up at 06.30—no mean feat on its own as Edan is a sleepyhead and the medication he is on makes him drowsy. Edan was now dressed, ready, and still on trial at work. Then there was me, desperately requiring time away from my son for just a few hours! What people don't always seem to see is the fact that disability is an inclusive journey. We *all* go through it. It's tiresome, often thankless, and can keep you on a permanent edge. In addition, I had my own mental illness to contend with.

Throughout the day, I had my eye on the time, expecting that dreadful call from his manager. Four o'clock came around, and no call—p*hew!* Edan had finished work and would be going to his bowling program until six in the evening. At bowling, he'd only had one episode outside the premises. That infernal radio's fault again, with its infernal 's' sounds and repetitive use of the number *six*.

I ventured out to collect Edan from the bowling alley, just as I had done hundreds of times before without an issue, grateful that morning's rage-a-holic episode held no bearing on his public behaviour. When I saw him leaving the front doors, he didn't look well. Stupidly, I asked him to go back in and say goodbye to Yanek. I should have taken him straight home. Oh, how many times I've told myself this ever since that fateful day. Edan came out, got inside the car, and before I could even turn my engine on, he began screaming and hitting his face and head uncontrollably. Then, in what felt like only a ten second period, if that, he was out of the car and my immediate reach, screaming and gesticulating like a madman, out and into the bowling alley's car park. Mel came out to assist me and I instructed her to go back inside, alert the owners of what was happening and keep everyone inside with the front doors locked. My corrections training again kicking in, thank goodness.

I thought that, without an audience, Edan would get back in the car and we could then hopefully get home, but instead I watched him turn around and run at a small group of children that had just walked past on the footpath. I saw a curly-haired boy literally run for his life as Edan chased the group across the road, screaming the most horrific threats at them including the only distinct words I heard my son say; "I want to kill an innocent person". I immediately called 000 to have the police arrive on the scene for assistance. Mel came out of the bowling alley, and I begged her to call the ambulance service while I answered 000's location and other questions.

As I was panicking on the phone, begging 000 to hurry the hell up, I saw Mel run in a westerly direction screaming "No, Edan, no!" and then I heard my own screams.

Edan had picked up a huge rock and proceeded to throw it through the rear window of an oncoming vehicle. As I heard the tyres screeching to a halt, the driver, a man, yelled out, "What are you fucking doing?"

Everything became a blur at that point. I still had 000 asking me questions and yet all I wanted to do was to run to these poor innocent people in order to assess the damage. Thank goodness for my beautiful, dear friend Mel, who took over the phone calls as I moved frantically between the victims of my son and Edan himself, who had now walked away from the scene and was sitting down being talked down by a disability support worker from the bowling program, who was, ironically, a retired cop. I knew Edan was over the worst of his rage and in good hands, so I completely ignored him. I think that at that point, I hated him and did not want him near me.

To my complete horror, I watched as two young children alighted from the vehicle, their mother tripping over and falling on her knees from shock, with an enraged father demanding answers. The younger of the two children, a little boy, had blood trickling from his upper arm, and his mother was now back on her feet, mopping the blood up with a hand towel. I could hear myself begging the strangers' forgiveness and hoping to reassure them that the police and ambulance had been called and were on their way. I could also hear myself telling them about Edan's autism, like it was some form of absolution from bad behaviour—but then with the same bated breath I asked for them to lay charges. Edan had to realise what he did was gaol worthy. Had that rock hit differently, this poor, unsuspecting, innocent child could have been killed!

Moments later, another SUV pulled up and an enraged woman alighted commanding; "Can someone tell me who this man is going around terrorising small children?"

I knew instantaneously who this woman was: the mother of the first lot of children Edan had chased and traumatised. My entire mother's world imploded. Look at what my son had done! This woman was ropable, and justifiably so. I was again calling 000 trying to give them the hurry up. It was half an hour now since both incidents, and although Edan continued sitting far from the scene with the former cop still talking to him, I wanted desperately for the authorities and ambulance to take him away. I wanted these parents vindicated so that they did not consider me an irresponsible human. I wanted Edan detained so I could find out what was going on for him, so I could get my old Edan back. If I was scared before, I was now horrified and a complete hostage to a higher level of dread.

This was Edan only the week before the dreaded dual meltdown that caused so many people grief. Edan had tried hard to cope at Yanek's sister's 21st birthday party, but after a couple of hours he asked me to take him home.

The woman who had just arrived was not interested in my apology. She was out for blood, and she was going to get it. When the police finally arrived, with the main officer being the same one who attended the Williamstown incident, the woman pushed past me demanding priority. Bruce directed his attention to Edan and then returned to me. By this time the ambulance had arrived, as had my husband. Mel was still my mouthpiece, as bit by bit my clarity and concentration deteriorated. I even yelled at the second parent. The ones whose car was hit were cooperating with both me and the police though, even deciding not to press charges because they felt empathy for us as they also had children on the spectrum. I actually begged them to and was relieved when the second woman *insisted* on doing so. It turned out one of the first children Edan had chased down was on the spectrum, as well as having been assaulted on the street by a stranger only six months before. The child and his siblings were on their way home from a Christmas concert at their school. The child in question had only *just* started to feel confident about going out in public without adult guardianship. Oh Edan… you actually did to one of your own kind what you were enraged about having happened to you.

As I watched the ambulance take Edan away once again, I didn't know what to feel or how to react. Mel went off to tell the bowling alley staff it was safe for everyone to come out and go home now, and I simply got into my car and disappeared.

Hospital

Edan spent three days in the emergency department. He was far too volatile to return to the mental health assessment unit, so the triage staff had to wait for a bed to become available in the 1G psychiatric unit. I did not call Edan this time. Firstly, he'd smashed his new phone, and secondly, I needed to be away from him. I'd worked in a large Sydney hospital before, and I knew Edan was safe where he was, so safe, in fact, that because of Edan's volatility, a security guard had been assigned to sit with him for most of the day.

My darling, patient, hero of a husband went to the hospital on day two to take some clean clothes to Edan. Edan was still in his bowling shirt and steel capped boots. As Adam walked past the rows of ED booths, some of his colleagues from the Adelaide Remand Centre who were guarding a prisoner caught sight of him and called him to them. Adam explained that he was there to visit his stepson. One of the guards then said, "Well just watch out, there's a guy somewhere along here who went ballistic and smashed his head open just a couple of hours ago."

That guy was Edan. When he was told he wasn't going to the comfy mental health assessment unit like the previous two times, he went crazy and smashed his head open by banging it repeatedly on the floor, resulting in a deep gash and another black eye.

Edan spent a total of seven weeks in the 1G psychiatric unit. Many of those around Edan were in a worse mental condition than he was. Most were much older than him. In 1G there was a lot of screaming, aimless walking around, and staring into space. A severely autistic girl was repeatedly self-harming and her eyes always looked as if they were bleeding. It was truly a scene from One Flew Over The Cuckoo's Nest. However, it was not as severe, thank God, as the psychiatric behaviour I'd seen many years before when I was a juvenile justice officer. I was grateful for this much, at least.

I visited Edan five times while he was in the psychiatric unit. The first time I found him crying helplessly over a tasteless sandwich. He begged me to not leave the unit without him. It took everything inside of me to tell him this would not be occurring. What he did was very serious and he was lucky he wasn't in gaol. Edan refuted my answer with a meltdown, running outside into the drab unit courtyard screaming. I left.

During the next two visits, Edan appeared settled and improved. I guess he had finally acclimatised. He asked for McDonald's and his pencils and art books. He began drawing again, although his drawings reflected some of the angry characters from his video games, particularly Marco Bartoli and his henchmen, from the Lara Croft games. Along with another character from the same game, Father Patrick Dunstan, who signified the struggle with the parochial institution that defines good and evil, sin and retribution. Abstract topics such as religion are not something Edan copes with very well. I'm wondering if it's a general rule of thumb for all Aspies, given their highly logical and literal perspective on everything. Inside the 1G, anything given to Edan required staff inspection and authorisation. This wasn't a boarding school; it was scheduled detainment for seriously ill patients.

Christmas Day came around and Adam visited Edan on his own, as I was working that day. I did, however, have a video call with Edan on Adam's phone to wish him a Merry Christmas. Edan's father also arrived to see his son for the first time since that dreadful October day, but Edan's reaction was not favourable. Edan caught sight of his father waiting for staff at reception and told Adam he did not wish to see him and to get him out of there. Even though it had been Edan who threw the first punch, he still deeply resented his father for goading him and punching him back. The way Edan saw things, it was his father's fault that Edan became so brutal, and he couldn't understand how a father could hit his own son.

Just before the end of December 2019, after begging staff at the 1G to review Edan's medications once more, Edan lost it over another patient telling him that he could not use a certain milk in the communal fridge. The ferocity of his actions, which included running at a duty nurse with threatening behaviour, landed Edan in the completely sterile 1F. In 1F, Edan could not even obtain a single pencil or his beloved tights (more on these later). Here, Edan finally realised how his behaviour was impacting his life. Edan was now scared and not so valiant. But the behavioural component, which the duty psychiatrist seemed convinced was Edan's primary problem, was not all there was to it and I'd had enough of waiting for tangible results. After watching Edan run at a wall with all his strength in his worn pyjamas in order to hurt himself and release frustration for not being allowed to return to 1G, I demanded immediate action regarding his medication. Six weeks in hospital was long enough to determine Edan's autistic defiance was not the only problem!

The following week, Adam and I had a conference with a variety of professionals including the duty psychiatrist, who now decided perhaps the drug given to Edan by the area psychiatrist for his OCD may have contributed to Edan's heightened emotional sensitivity and rages. I sighed with relief and broke down in tears. Just moments before, I had declared my son homeless if the hospital discharged him without a medication review. I was not putting my family, Edan, or the public in further danger. It's not as though our prisons are free of prisoners living with Asperger's syndrome or autism: many prisoners present as being on the spectrum, to some degree. Suffering from mental illness or a mental developmental disorder such as ASD does not make the perpetrator immune to ending up in gaol, alas. Our mental health system is terribly underfunded with precious few resources, and so many people just like Edan fall through the cracks of medical care, landing in custodial services instead.

On the ninth of January 2020, only four days after the Paroxetine was removed from Edan's medication list, we were asked to take Edan home. I couldn't keep Edan in hospital anymore. He was now responding better than ever before to directives and routines, and as much as I had relished my relative freedom at home without Edan and his problems, it was time to get him back and to put in place serious anti-anxiety preventers and blockers.

The mother who had pursued charges against Edan had not dropped them, and while Edan was in hospital, the officers on Edan's case had paid us a visit to ascertain that we agreed Edan's actions were caused by his intellectual disability.

Adam and I concurred, and the officers were satisfied that to continue further would not be fair to Edan or us. The police therefore overrode Edan's accuser. I reached out to both sets of parents on a Facebook community chat page for our area to extend my heartfelt apologies, given I did not know these parents' names. The mother of the children walking home from their Christmas school concert slandered me as an attention-seeking fraud, adding that knowing my son was a risk, why did I allow him to attend a public program. She also stated that I was now conveniently 'advertising' my fake apology to promote a book launch I had organised at the public library for my self-published autobiography. This parent concluded with the all too predictable hope that one day, karma would find me and teach me my lesson. In sharp contrast, the mother of the child hit by Edan's rock added me on Facebook and we've now become friends, with this kind soul even going as far as to borrow my autobiography to read.

Edan on his way home from hospital on the 9th of January. Almost seven weeks as a mental health ward scheduled patient. The first thing he asked for was takeaway pizza. His drawings began to take on a sinister consistency henceforth.

Hospital Separation Summary

Allied Health Notes

Edan's Paroxetine was tapered off and stopped, as the high dose could have been contributing to his aggression. His OCD symptoms remained stable. It was thought that this might have been the underlying cause of his aggression.

We were happy to have him back home. We had expressed the wish for Edan to transition into independent living in the long-term future, as we had plans to move overseas on retirement. This, in addition to recent attempts Edan was making to satisfy his sexual needs by cross-dressing, seemed to contribute to his current situation.

On discharge, Edan presented as calm, cooperative, and polite. He was grateful for the treating team's efforts. His speech was appropriate, with no suicidal, delusional, or aggressive themes. He was future-focused. His affect was euthymic. He was alert and orientated, with his insight and judgement intact. Rapport had been reestablished.

The Great Aftermath

Over the next few months Adam and I devised various strategies that would hopefully minimise or control Edan's spikes in anxiety-fuelled rages. First on the list was the complete elimination of free or unsupervised access to the internet. All video games of a violent nature were confiscated. Videos were to have non-violent themes, namely the Disney types which were encouraged and purchased for him en masse. Walking around the vineyard and surrounding land became a must, and, until Edan could return to work, time spent at home included varying degrees of quiet, reflective time utilising guided meditation, and the free use of his tights. We also ordered custom-made noise-cancelling ear plugs for him: one set at 50% noise cancelling; and the second set at 90% for the most difficult of times. Peripheral sounds that disturbed Edan enough to cause meltdowns were many, alas.

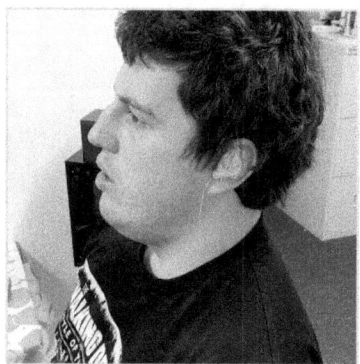

Edan being fitted for noise cancelling ear plugs by an audiologist.

While Edan was in the hospital mental health assessment unit for the second time, I went to see a local spiritual healer in order to restore some inner peace to my mind and body. I make no secret about being a practicing metaphysician and spiritualist. I explained to the healer why I was there, and the turmoil my son had experienced and inadvertently passed on to us. We spoke at length about Edan's spiritual purpose and how it tied in with his disability. At the end of the session, the healer informed me that Edan would be revealing something that would make a great difference to his life.

The very next week, following Edan's discharge, I was at the sink washing the dishes when Edan stormed into the kitchen and unequivocally stated that he had something to tell me and I had better just accept it!

Edan disclosed what may best be described as a tights and stockings fetish. Apparently, he'd had it for many, many years, from as young as seven or eight years of age. I had no idea. I had found said items stashed away in his room once or twice, but I thought it was just due to silly banter with his sisters who often dressed him up when he was a little boy, as all big sisters do.

Edan, aged six and dressed up as Snow White by his sisters. These seemingly innocent viccisitudes may have sown the seed of fetishism into Edan.

I often wondered how Edan dealt with sexual desire, however this manifested itself, given that Edan is adamant he is not interested in having a girlfriend or having sex with another human being. Now I knew.

Edan finds sexual release by wearing his tights. He completes the setting by also wearing a G-string, a padded bra, and a girl's tank top. Edan lies perfectly still on his bed, concentrating on how his tights feel, and wills an orgasm this way without once touching his penis. The entire effort can take hours, but it is in fact a deep form of meditation for him, very calming, and something I absolutely do not discourage, and even suggest to Edan if he is feeling out of sorts sometimes. When Edan told me about the tights I let out a sigh of relief. I was happy for him. I worried that a great deal of his nervous tension had something to do with sexual suppression. This was actually great news for us all!

Edan and I have had many discussions about his tights since that disclosure day. He explained how he used to sneak out his sister's black school tights and wear them to bed where he wouldn't be found out, or any time he had the chance. Edan had even rummaged through my drawers. Of course, this now meant he had to have his own stash, and so we went shopping together, the whole time appearing very discreet around other shoppers, because even though Edan defended his right to be who he was and to like what he liked, he was well aware that public opinion wouldn't always be sympathetic. Edan was very specific about the colour, denier, and fit of the tights, even researching these at length on the internet—supervised of course. The healer had obviously seen this coming, and I was extremely grateful.

All stakeholders who received any contact with Edan, including his father, his family, his best friend, and so on, were given a 'DOs and DON'Ts' list to which they had to strictly adhere.

When I worked as a disability support worker I had a client who was transitioning from male to female. This client was very brave, finally coming out as her true self at the age of fifty-seven, in a community that could be quite close minded to such things. I remember always walking just a step faster than her, so as to partially shield her from glaring stares, given that she still looked very much male in her women's attire. I'd also talk to her and have her look at me so she herself did not catch the stares and have a meltdown. This is how hyper vigilant and protective I've now become with my own son; always pre-empting or hoping to predict the public stressors whenever I've taken him out, which has not been often at all since his major meltdown, and as a result of the COVID-19 restrictions.

The not for profit disability support organisation that Edan worked for failed him miserably, too. I say 'too' because it took threats, tears, and time for the hospital staff to realise Edan's behaviour was not merely behavioural as they suggested and, for a considerable time, actively insisted on. The supported employee services manager had promised Edan a return to work trial, based on a wealth of supporting evidence, which deemed Edan safe to return to a factory environment. We worked really hard to provide this evidence. One item was a rather pointed letter from Edan's psychologist, which explained how a return to normal routine after a three-month absence would actually be highly beneficial for his mental health and subsequent rehabilitation. I had also sent Edan to a camp for people living with a disability with his best friend Yanek. Although the experience itself did not go down too well, because the support workers were less than proactive—with one even calling an autistic man an 'asshole' because he was habitually noisy, Edan had managed to control his anger whilst there. He did, however, unleash his frustration upon returning home and stated in no uncertain terms that he would never return to this venue or he'd assault the insensitive support worker.

Camp Report By Supervisor

Edan participated well throughout the camp, and engaged in all the chosen activities. This included two beach visits, cooking a BBQ at the beach, cycling around the farm and feeding the animals. Throughout the duration of the camp Edan was very polite and didn't demonstrate any behaviours of concern. He was helpful for the staff and supported the other participants with the activities. He was most helpful when on the trips to the beach and engaged really well with cooking the BBQ. Edan followed his routines very well, and there was no apparent issue if the routine had to be adjusted due to time constraints. Edan was compliant when asked to perform a certain job or activity, which enabled the days to run smoother and allowed for a more purposeful experience. We did observe Edan stand up for himself when firmly instructed to come down from climbing a piece of equipment at the park. Edan did not become aggressive, but simply stated he had the capacity to spend time on it. Edan would be welcome to come back to the group as all staff found him to be kind, supportive, and friendly with both staff and other participants.

After the major bowling alley incident, the organisation that employed Edan (and also employed me as a support worker) went into immediate damage control, which I understood and accepted. But what they did not explain, and which I found out via other means and did not accept, was that they took advantage of this traumatic event in our lives to unceremoniously kick Edan out of the job he'd known and worked in efficaciously for almost five years (I was with the organisation for eight years and was also not always treated fairly) due to a change in pay scale versus productivity. This means that the stipulations they had set out for Edan, which we complied with to the letter, were not honoured because they'd already decided Edan was not going to fit these pay scale and productivity guidelines. This was additionally confirmed to me when other not so productive supported employees were moved sideways out of the factory some had known all their working lives (the organisation was established in the 70's) into a money-making (for the organisation alone) 'leisure program'.

Edan's Return To Work Plan (February 2020)

To commence initially with working two hours/day, as negotiated with my SES Manager.

Ideally this would be before Edan's scheduled holiday in April 2020

To increase hours incrementally when we agree (me, my manager, my mum, my psychologist, and my doctor) I feel comfortable and I am ready to do so.

Coping Skills: Things I can do to stay calm

- If I think about something I don't like (e.g. nasty people, the internet) I will say to myself:
  - Don't listen to those thoughts.
  - Those thoughts are trying to taunt me and they are being bullies.
  - I don't have to listen. If I'm at home I can listen to something else e.g. a helpful meditation CD.
- Having only one instruction at a time is very helpful. Please don't overload me.
- Having other people speak to me in a calm, kind voice is helpful.
- I can wear my noise-cancelling ear plugs when it is safe to do so. I can tell my supervisor when I am using these so they can be aware of it.
- If I feel anxious, angry or upset at work, I can:
  - tell a supervisor I need time out.
  - take up to 20 minutes of time out, and then I can decide whether I can return to work or whether I need another 10 minutes, and I will let my supervisor know.
- If I still feel upset or angry, I can ask to go home for the rest of the day or I will sit in the outside area, or I'll wait for mum to pick me up from an agreed location.
- It is really helpful if people let me calm down independently without talking to me, so I can self-regulate and return when I know I am ready.

Social Support: People I Can Talk To At Work

- My supervisor.
- SES Manager.

External Support: Things Other People Can Do That Will Help Me

- Mum and Adam will keep helping me stay safe at home.
- Keep regular appointments with my psychologist and my doctor.
- Keep watching nice movies.
- Stay away from looking up negative things on the internet.
- Mum will help me tell Dad what I need to stay calm (e.g. minimise criticism, not encouraging me to fight) and Mum will write things down for him.
- I will only spend a little bit of time with Dad while I am still focused on getting healthier.
- I will exercise regularly at home - walking or jumping.

Edan and co-worker, 'Colin'. A beautiful friendship which ended when Edan had to leave the supported employment workshop.

Given all of the above, including the $238 psychologist's report that was requested by the SES Manager as part of the evidence required for a work trial, it made sense for Edan to be given another chance at his job, keeping in mind it was now two months after his discharge from hospital. This was, after all, a disability support services organisation that prided itself on individual assessment and support. The SES Manager, who in actual fact had a score to settle with me from a long time before when she was my manager, decided to screen Edan on his own (something I considered completely unethical), asking him questions which no doubt elicited the answers which would then arm her with a work trial deferral, therefore negating the intention of a work trial! An Aspie always tells it as he/she sees it, and the SES manager knew this only too well.

Unwilling to put Edan or myself through another gratuitous merry-go-round with a woman who had no intention of keeping her promise, I declined a referral to a second interview 'after Edan returns from holiday' (the holiday was cancelled due to COVID-19), and submitted his resignation by proxy, pointedly denouncing both the SES manager and the organisation who silently backed her.

Only a few weeks later, after almost eight years of service as a disability support worker, as I had returned to the job after six weeks working as a school janitor, I also resigned. I just couldn't bring myself to look at those managers in the eye again without feeling white-hot flames of hatred and outrage. Supporting vulnerable people my ass!

Where was my poor son to work now? And he was so going to miss his friends.

Edan's fetishism became acknowledged by a psychiatrist as part of his overall diagnosis.

Edan and I got to work on various coping strategies. I needed to change the tone of my voice considerably. I had been raised by a neurotic narcissist, and the spirited attitude I learned from her had to go. This change would ultimately benefit me and my marriage, as well as my relationship with Edan. As a family, we needed to be very aware of what we would talk about in front of—and to—Edan. The 'DOs and DON'Ts' list was the best guideline for this. Positive reinforcement was the key. Edan had to be given 'Power of Attorney' over himself and his reactions. I had Edan draw up a contract and self-management guidelines list, which he titled 'My Promise to the Family'. in order for him to exercise choice, control, and self-governance.

When Edan was doing the Tomatis method, his practitioner recommended we purchase Edan a Forbrain headset, stating how speaking via this device is a form of bone conductor brain training, which greatly benefits children on the autism spectrum. Once per week, while I do my ironing, Edan sits in front of me for up to an hour, reading from his Harry Potter books or from a film or video script he finds online, while wearing his Forbrain.

Despite these Forbrain sessions being very calming for Edan, and great mother/son time, Edan's soothing monotone also puts Conan (our Pomeranian) to sleep.

Treating Edan's anxiety was now paramount, and a definite priority—over and above social facilitation and acceptance of his Asperger's. Edan had become a ticking time bomb before his hospital admission and we were still far from feeling comfortable that at any given moment that bomb wouldn't go off. COVID-19 and it's 'stay at home' restrictions did not offer us the opportunity to trial community reengagement practices, and so Edan and our family had little choice but to cocoon ourselves into a pupa of unreality, indefinitely tucked away, deep in the safety and anonymity of our socially disconnected vineyard.

OCD

The removal of the Paroxetine from Edan's medication regime meant his OCD behaviours escalated, and quickly. Whereas before he was able to suppress them to a certain extent, then get to boiling point and explode, now he indulged in their tiresome routines to their fullest. As frustrating and disruptive as they are, I prefer them to what we were dealing with previously.

When I went to see Professor Tony Attwood at the Barossa Valley seminar on Valentine's Day 2020 and he spoke about all of the behaviour characteristics experienced by people living with Asperger's syndrome and ASD, among the dozens of topics discussed was his aversion to antidepressant medication (i.e. Paroxetine). Professor Attwood explained he did not experience many harmonious results between the two things… bingo! I was never putting Edan on them again, OCD or no OCD. During the packed seminar, I truly felt Professor Attwood only spoke to me (and yes I did have front row seats). Edan was everything that was discussed in some form or another. I realised once more the sets of complexities we all suffered under—all of us, but principally Edan. To be Edan and not want to take your own life must be a very courageous thing, and statistics show so many young people on the spectrum do.

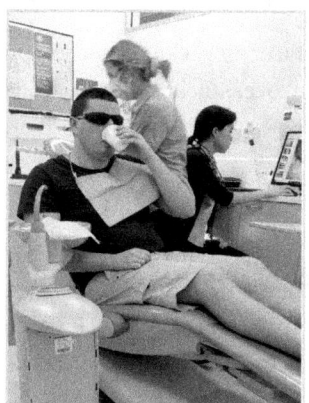

Edan, well overdue dentist's appointment (due to his mental breakdown and frequent hospitalisations). I had to brief the dentist on how to approach Edan and whether she would switch off the overhead television set to avoid triggers, and close the door so Edan would not hear others speaking in reception or along the corridor.

It takes Edan up to ten minutes to get through his extensive OCD routine before he can begin or end a task. It is exasperating to watch and hear, and highly testing. I continue to jump through hoops to avoid the Mr Hyde of December 6th 2019, and both accept and defend these routines. To me it's undoubtedly the lesser of two evils and it appears Edan's way of self-regulation is as good as it gets—for now at least. Historically, Edan has dropped one habit or OCD behaviour, only to begin a new one. As it stands, there are no clear-cut therapies or medications that effectively treat severe OCD. Although he is treated by a very talented and relatable clinical psychologist, Edan's cognitive behavioural therapy isn't going anywhere. He'll sit in the psychologist's room agreeing with and acknowledging everything she tells him, and literally the second we leave her building, he has to release his suppressed demons via his OCD routines.

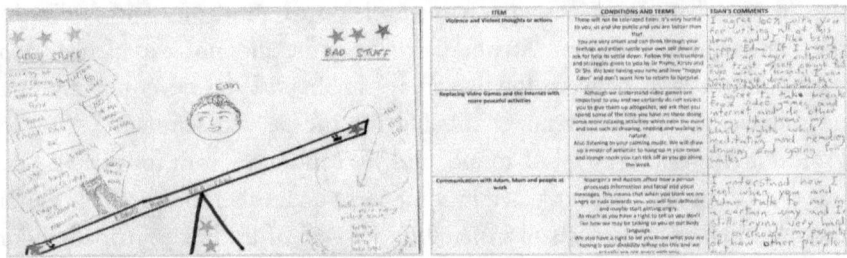

One of the many behaviour management tools Edan's psychologist has worked with him on. This is laminated and stuck at eye level in his bedroom for him to review.

We are currently looking at another 'supported employee' factory-environment organisation over an hour away from us for Edan to hopefully work in for only two days a week. The three days per week in which Edan participated over the past five years is too much hyper-sensory stimulation. On his third 'not-at-home' day, we have Edan attend a leisure options group in Gawler with another close friend and former colleague,. In fact, Edan will only attend if his friend attends.

During a third capacity-building interview at this second prospective place of employment where Edan was practically done with the eligibility and entry formalities and was now being risk-assessed for the next step of work experience, Edan had a meltdown and threw a chair across the room at a white board. The email I sent his careers organiser (who was not the person who had sparked Edan's reaction) will give an overview of why Edan lost control, although he had a hold on his temper for close to five months.

Hi B,

To begin with, I apologise profusely to both you and J for what happened today. It was inexcusable, and both Edan and I are extremely sorry.

Secondly, please send me a bill for the chair. I saw debris on the ground so I know something was broken. The organisation does not need to pay for the actions of others.

Thirdly, please understand that the line of questioning and reassurance J was aiming to obtain was the problem today. Each time I approach a new stakeholder for Edan I talk to them first and attempt to coach them on how to talk to Edan. In the same way a disabilities manager needs to mould themselves to their clients on an individual basis in order to get the best outcome. This approach comes from my experience as a disability support worker, and not as a protective mother hen. I was under the distinct impression I had explained what upsets Edan when I first called you at the very beginning of this journey.

Edan has Asperger's with high anxiety, but he is also a polite and conscientious young man willing to work and make friends—this I can guarantee you. I understand your risk assessment protocols and that they need to be followed and presented, but as Edan told me in the car after we left, it sounded like J was pushing the point that Edan **had to accept** these, with little interference from supervisors. He just felt it was going to be like his former place of employment all over again, where harassment was rife and supported employees weren't reined in for poor behaviour. Edan has been bullied and forced to endure certain situations for long enough, and why shouldn't he be assured he won't have to suffer harassment?

Ideally, it would have been nice if we'd had a tour of the factory and for Edan to be able to come to his own decision about whether he'd like the job or no,t with a few gentle recommendations from J. This would have elicited a completely different outcome. Edan felt he was being given ultimatums and indisputable conditions. Disability support is about flexibility and individual tailoring. As J's line of questioning continued, I so wanted to pull the plug on the meeting because, based on past situations, I felt what did in fact transpire was inevitable. I know my son and his stressors really well now.

I don't know if you're happy to give Edan another try. He is willing to try again with you—this he has unequivocally stated. Please let me know before I begin the tiresome job of looking for another employer for him. He's too young and talented to stay home doing nothing.

Please would you call or reply back to this email at your earliest convenience. Additionally, please apologise on our behalf to your supported employees, receptionist, and staff that may have heard or witnessed the fracas. We are both extremely ashamed of any poor impression or feelings of concern that it instilled.

Ideally, and by his own admission, Edan would better suit outdoor work, as say a landscaper's assistant, or as part of a small gardening team. The type of foreman Edan would relate to is a neurotypical without ego, who'll listen to our recommendations, and the fact that the NDIS was supposedly created to cater to individuals and is not a 'one size fits all' modus operandi, as we've so far experienced with these assisted-employee organisations.

The meltdown meant that Edan was required to participate in a positive behaviour plan course before the new organisation could proceed with his application. More anxiety for us, as we feared more insensitive communication approaches towards Edan.

I will now close with a letter that Edan wrote to me while scheduled as a mental health patient in the 1G ward. This letter proves Edan has a good heart and is as accountable for his actions as the next person. It's just his Asperger's that gets in his way, and the way some experts see ASD these days, Asperger's is actually a gift… just try telling this to those who have to support the gifted individual. I certainly have my days where I ask myself, "What would I do with just *one* wish?"

Edan's Letter from the 1G Mental Health Ward

December 2019, age 23

Dear Mum,

What you just wrote to me on this paper made me feel really depressed, made me feel like absolute shit about myself that someone like me with autism wood (sic) hurt their own kind, honestly, I didn't know until you told me in this letter, I feel so shit and disgusted and betrayal about myself and I feel like a piece of shit to the parents of the kids.

The parents have every right to be mad at me for worrying about kids because they don't know I'm disabled too or my life-story, they don't even know me in person. And I feel so incredibly sorry for the huge cut I gave that woman who turned out to be your friend on FB and who understands disabilities, and even the kids in the same car as her were autistic and I nearly could have killed them!

I really do appreciate you letting me know about the details of what I've done and the consequences like cancelling America and all that, but it really didn't unbrighten my mood because I was just starting to be happy and calm and myself again at this ward I'm at now.

But no one to blame though and I do hope when three years have passed then you and Adam would still feel good for the opportunity to do the American, Canada, and Alaskan trip to make up for missing out on April next year because I'm really sad that especially I can't go now. I feel like I don't want you to come and visit me this Sunday because I know when I see your face I get really sad and I don't even want to look at it thinking how could I break such a sweet heart who is my own loving, caring mum's heart and even when I don't want to look at your face I feel really sorry for myself too with all the things I've been through.

That's why I started to get angry when both you and Adam came for the meeting at this ward because I knew you were angry too and I couldn't handle seeing you when I still wasn't in a good position. I'm really sorry if that sounded too harsh to you but it's all my honesty. I love you and if you still want and decide to visit me on Sunday that's fine. I just thought we should still have a break from each other for longer until I'm allowed to go back home and I see you at home instead, and I decided that, NOT you okay? But anyway, your decision.

Love Edan

xxx

EPILOGUE

Edan on his experience as a scheduled mental health patient, his black tights, what he enjoys doing, and the differences between neurotypicals and people living with Asperger's syndrome, being a child and an adult – Interview conducted on March 15th 2020

Mum: *Okay, Edan, tell me how you felt when you stayed at the Lyell McEwan Hospital (1G mental health unit).*

Edan: *Well, I felt, I guess I felt a bit different. I felt okay some of the time I was there, but also I felt a bit down some of the time I was there. A bit angry, sad and, and also I felt very homesick, and I missed my family and friends while I was there and all that.*

Mum: *Okay… if you were to go in there again, how would you feel?*

Edan: *I'd feel bad all over again because I'd feel like, after I got released a second time I'd go to prison or something?*

Mum: *Why would you feel you'd go to prison?*

Edan: *Well I don't know if I'd feel like that for sure, but last time, my psychologist at the Lyle McEwan, Doctor Michael, said if something like that happened again, of what I did back at bowling, the next thing that would happen is I'd have to go to court and the judge would say it would not be seen as a mental health problem, and I'd go straight to prison.*

Mum: *Oh okay. So, do you think something like that is ever going to happen again?*

Edan: *No.*

Mum: *Okay, and tell me what do you think your future looks like from now on?*

Edan: *I think my future looks like it would go to the right path, and it would find itself going into the right path, and it would release any big problem that I would have in the past and any big problem I would have in the future, and if I keep trying and trying to make the most of my life it would make my life pretty much all, good and all productive and happy.*

Mum: *Okay. And what do you really want for your future?*

Edan: *I want to, I want to keep up with, I want to keep up my new jobs now that I'm going to have instead of having too many people around me that give me too many issues, where there's lots of noisy areas and stuff and I want to keep up playing around with my hobbies.*

Mum: *(Interrupts) So you don't want to keep up with your former workplace anymore?*

Edan: *No.*

Mum: *So you want to work just one-on-one?*

Edan: *Yes, just one-on-one.*

Mum: *Well, what sort of hobbies do you really enjoy?*

Edan: *Well, one of them is probably the usual most people with Asperger's like, video games and stuff and also, and also, also I like, I really like going swimming and I guess also hanging out with my friends, and playing with the dogs, walking the dogs. And also eating, I enjoy eating my favourite foods.*

Mum: *Which are your favourite foods?*

Edan: *Well my top favourite food would have to be pasta, because... how much Italian am I?*

Mum: *A quarter.*

Edan: *A quarte... a quarter of Italian because my mum is... how much Italian are you?*

Mum: *Half.*

Edan: *Because my mum is half Italian, and we have half Italian in the family, and I like all types of pastas... I like pesto, spaghetti and meatballs, and Carbonara, and spaghetti Bolognaise, and um... is there another one I like? Oh yeah and pasta with cut up pieces of salami in it with the normal red pasta sauce, with olives and all that in them, and that's my top favourite food.*

Mum: *Okay, now tell me about this, if you were to meet someone who didn't know anything about Asperger's syndrome, how would you describe yourself to them? What is it about Asperger's syndrome that people need to know?*

Edan: *Well, the thing about Asperger's syndrome… still being on the topic about, about my hobbies and all that, apparently I have this hobby where I like to wear women's black tights, because apparently kids that have Autism and Asperger's syndrome have like, have like this type of liking or fetish where they like this texture on their skin and it kind of makes them sort of have like this sexual feeling even if they're not, even if they have not reached puberty yet… is it okay to talk about the sperm?*

Mum: *Yes.*

Edan: *Where it's not like the proper way to let out sperm yet but instead of proper I could use a more grown up word… and there's a lot of guys out there… my mum looked up in the internet and it said there's a lot of male genders out there who like to wear stockings, and they aren't gay, they're still straight. And apparently my mum told me that they like wearing tights because they find it, when they think about that women like to wear them they like to wear them as well, so it makes the … it makes them… um, how would I describe it?*

Mum: *Feel sexy?*

Edan: *Cos they probably like it when other women wear them so they can have the same advantages as women, and the same sensation of wearing them, the same texture on their skin. And that's the type of theory that I like about wearing the black tights because I find that I'm not gay, but I do find women attractive, and even the ones that don't wear them I find attractive, but when they do wear them I find them more attractive, because when I see them wearing them I find it very sexy because when I see them wearing them, it gives me that feeling. And the reason I like them so much is I find the colour black a sexy colour, even my mum told me that people find red a sexy colour, but I find black a sexy colour because there's um… could you help me out sometimes Mum?*

Mum: *Well, it's just because you like the colour black, because you find it sexy.*

Edan: *Yes, that's right, and I think it has a lot to do with other people wearing fashionable clothes that are not tights but like black too. And my favourite types of tights are the very high number denier ones. The very thick winter ones, because the thicker the tights the sexier they feel and the more they* have a heavier feel. My mum says most of the men on the internet like the sheer tights but I like the thicker ones because I think they feel a bit stronger on me and I like, I like having the areas of the thickness around the crotch and the buttocks. And sometimes there's times when it makes me, I don't always wear the tights for sexual reasons, they also help me with my depression and anger and my sadness.

Mum: So how do they help you with anger and depression?

Edan: Because they're like a type of relief… it's still for a sexual reason, but because I have been wearing them since I was a little kid and before I told my mum I had a fetish for black tights, I used to do this thing when I was a little kid where I used to go through my older sister's drawers when she wore black tights to high school, and I'd put them on whenever anyone was not home, and I'd put them on by myself or if everyone was out in another room watching a movie and I was just in my room by myself doing my own thing, I'd put them on and then if I heard someone coming I'd get under the blankets because that's how addicted I was to them. I was really obsessed with black tights because I wanted, I wanted… because that's my type of way of having the experience of sex, because I never wanted to have a relationship with an actual woman, because I never really wanted one, and I still don't because I think it's too difficult for a person like me with Asperger's and I think, I prefer tights over women. I see tights as a type of relationship, and I see tights as my best friend, and see them as someone that doesn't leave you, and doesn't judge you, and doesn't argue with you or force you to do things, it just loves you and likes being put on by someone that likes wearing them, and that's me. And oh, and because I wanted the experience of what sex feels like, I found that tights do the job, and I like to do this thing where I lie on my bed and, just relax. Sometimes I meditate while wearing them. I put meditation CD's on the stereo, and I close my eyes and there are times if I think about sexy stuff, the sperm comes out all the way out and as soon as it happens it feels amazing and it's a very good feeling, and all of that has is part of my recovery for my depression, anxiety, and sadness about the hardships I've had in life.

Mum: Do you feel ever since you told your parents about the tights, and you feel freer to do it, that your life has improved?

Edan: Um yeah I think my life has improved that I told my parents about it. I didn't tell every single member of my family bbecause I'm worried that some of the members of my family won't understand me properly or they'll

	judge me, and won't understand, and they'll think it's weird, but to me it's something very special. In my opinion it's something that I need that will help me improve my life, this relationship that I have with my tights, with this type of clothing that I like.
Mum:	*How many times a week do you use your tights?*
Edan:	*During daytime and night-time, after dinner or after I have my shower— several times a week. I even wear them in the bath because I watch videos on YouTube about people wearing them in the bath tub and getting them wet, and when they do that it kind of, it kind of starts to make me feel sexy in the crotch.*
Mum:	*Okay, let's change the subject and go back to the other question. If someone were to say to you, 'What the hell is Asperger's syndrome?' What would you say this means to you and who you are…? What makes you different because you have Asperger's?*
Edan:	*I think I would describe it, that Asperger's is people that think very differently to other people. That have very different ways to how they choose things, the way they talk and all that, and I think they have their special way of expressing their feelings to other people when they talk about things they are interested in, like things that they like and things they don't like, or things that they're afraid of or things that they're um… what else*
Mum:	*Okay, how are you different from someone who doesn't have Asperger's?*
Edan:	*Um, cos I think someone who hasn't got Asperger's, they just are like everyone else that sort of has their own proper way of how they act, and express themselves, and they just have an easier way of dealing with life, just like everyone else that doesn't have a disability or Asperger's, or autism and stuff like that.*
Mum:	*Do you wish you were someone who didn't have Asperger's?*
Edan:	*In my opinion not really because I think I prefer to have Asperger's than not have it because I think it's an easier life and I think because I have Asperger's there are things that I like and I don't like that are very easy to deal with and also, I think having Asperger's makes life feel easier. I don't like the idea of having a hard life.*
Mum:	*But sometimes you have a hard life now, like before you went to the Lyle McEwan and during.*

Edan: *Yeah, but I mean things that are hard to do when you don't have Asperger's. I can't really think of anything at the moment…*

Mum: (Intercepting) *Like when you go to the bank?*

Edan: *Like when you go to the bank and stuff and like when you try to find certain jobs, and having to make big explanations and stuff, and also trying to find a wife or a husband depending on what gender you are, I think it's too hard.*

Mum: *So you like being on your own?*

Edan: *Yes, I like being on my own… having my black tights as my partner instead.*

Mum: *Okay, this is the last question. How do you think you have changed from being a small boy into a young man as you are now? How do you see the changes in your life?*

Edan: (Having some OCD self-soothing noises for 20 seconds) *Um, I think my biggest changes are, that ever since I was young originally living interstate, that I have matured more, I understand more about life and I make wise decisions, and I express myself, I explain things more properly, and I have become a lot more wiser in my adulthood than I was in my childhood because when you are a child, you don't understand much and all you do, all you do is just play and muck around a lot because a child doesn't have the full understanding of an adult, they don't have that experience, and that goes with all children that grow up into adults, even those ones who don't have Asperger's. They all grow up, that's part of life and humanity, they grow up to understand more and stuff as they get older.*

Mum: *Do you like being grown up or did you prefer being a child?*

Edan: *I like being grown up, now that I'm not afraid to talk about things with my loved ones and stuff, I think it's easier being an adult, it's easy being a child but part of the easier part of being an adult is to tell them the truth and not lie about things, to let them know what your interests and worries are so that they can help you, and they can accept them, and all that so I like that part of being an adult.*

Mum: *Okay. So is that all you want to talk about today?*

Edan: *Yes.*

Mum: *Thank you.*

Edan: *That's okay.*

✳ ✳ ✳ ✳ ✳

Edan has been residing in supported independent living accommodation since December 2021.

The first disability services company to deal with Edan's monumental meltdowns encompassing serious property damage (including Edan's own personal belongings), assaulting staff and threatening the public, absconding, self-harm, suicidal ideation and suicide attempts, repeated police intervention, and frequent admissions to hospital, were amiable and wonderful to deal with, but unfortunately not strong enough to keep Edan in their care.

The second and current company fared just as poorly, but with the assistance of a dedicated and intuitive behaviour therapist and an almost weekly fight by us and Edan's coordinator for added medical and administrative interventions and funding, we have Edan in a much better place than before. This disability service's structure lends itself to stricter boundaries and SIL guidelines whilst still maintaining the dignity of their clients and observing the restrictive practices policies, which more often than not hold everyone at ransom, alas. The problem with Edan's situation is that, on top of a highly defined disability, he is also presenting with clear mental health issues and the national disability insurance scheme (NDIS) is a service which caters *only* for disability, so that when mental illness presents, it's almost impossible getting the same type of funding or implementing guidelines that deal with mental health illness—this includes the implementation of restrictive practices.

As of August 2022, Edan is receiving a depot injection each fortnight, which is a slow release anti-psychotic. So far, this depot injection appears to be working in the reduction and control regarding the number of destructive and manic behaviours, and this also going hand-in-hand with staff training, regarding special day-to-day client management.

The first house Edan took up residence in with the second disability services company was completely trashed by Edan and no longer habitable. Edan's new residence is considered 'robust housing' and harder to trash, but then Edan took his frustrations out on staff vehicles.

During one hospital admission last year, Edan started drawing on the walls in his hospital room, something he'd never done before. This behaviour was carried on to his live-in accommodation whenever mania hit him.

Edan's NDIS funding was reviewed three times during a short period of time because his destructive behaviour was going from really bad to horrific. To offer perspective, his old plan of many years went from approximately $130.000 p.a. to $700.000, released in September 2022. Further funding is still being sought by the Exceptional Needs Unit of the NDIA, in order to place Edan in Specialist Disability Accommodation, to further modify and fortify his new home against property damage, and also to maintain the current twenty four hour 2:1 carer support which utilises one carer remaining active during the night, as Edan does not often sleep through the night, spending a great deal of it drawing, then sleeping most of the next day. The total bill estimated for this is around $1.2 million per annum.

In the past eight months Edan has been Tasered by police, absconded for almost fifteen hours which almost sparked a missing persons press release, smashed at least eight television sets (two worth almost $2,000 each), just as many mobile phones if not more, all of his expensive gaming consoles, countless windows, caused extreme property and appliance damage, shattered the confidence of many of his carers, and hurt himself too many times to list here.

Adam and I have beseeched, through various mediums, the newly appointed South Australian Premier and the Minister for Health for help—particularly in the areas dealing with psychiatry and phamacogenetics. After literally calling every psychiatrist in the state and being told either their books were closed or Edan's issues did not fit in with their skill set, we were at a loss as to how Edan's medications could be analysed and changed, given most GPs could not reassign or modify medications without psychiatric counsel. The hospital's minor changes were not helping Edan, and more often than not he was being discharged too early to establish any pattern of behaviour that would warrant a more in depth psychiatric evaluation by any hospital expert who wasn't just a duty clinician serving at any given time during Edan's multiple admissions.

Finally, Edan was referred to an outpatient's community office, where a psychiatrist diagnosed Edan with Cluster B Personality Disorder and the relatively new subgroup ASD affliction coined Pathological Demand Avoidance. These diagnoses offered his behaviour therapy team new starting points in the ongoing management training and advice offered to accommodation staff, family, and anyone else coming into contact with Edan on a daily basis.

Edan's world has shrunk exponentially. Everything which once had him living a quasi-normal life has almost completely disappeared. It got to the point where Edan could no longer watch a movie, Disney animations included, ordering me to remove his vast DVD collection because just reading their cover blurb could trigger a damaging meltdown. Currently, Edan has very little contact with the public. He wears earmuffs almost all of the time to avoid triggering conversations and words, and spends the majority of his time in his room, drawing, listening to music, sleeping, or playing video games. His hygiene is questionable and staff need to choose their requests and wording very carefully, as do his family and team of professionals.

Edan has re-connected with his father, but there are no home visits or sleepovers. In fact, all family visits are to be booked in and pre-approved by Edan's service provider's house manager. Edan's structure is meticulously monitored and restructured as the need arises.

The health minister replied to our email seven months after writing, only to point out we had been 'successful in finding Edan the help he needs'. We are now in the process of a rebuttal to parliament, with the kind assistance of an area MP, which highlights that the help is still lacking in other areas and what we did achieve was via non-governmental input but due to hard and consistent work applied by Edan's extraordinary team of professionals.

Following a terrible and unprecedented assault by Edan on his lifelong friend Yanek in April 2022, Edan will not be allowed contact with him for a very long time. Edan is often regretful of his actions, claiming not to be able to control them once that 'on switch' has been flicked. Unfortunately for Edan, the 'on switch' comes with serious consequences, not only for Edan, but those around him too.

Edan's primary coping mechanism nowadays is to escape into a fictional world of his making called *Celco*. All of Edan's drawings depict various facets of this world. Edan lines the walls of his room with these depictions.

Celco is everything our 'wretched Earth' isn't, and any competition with or criticism of Celco will be met with a terrible and destructive meltdown. Edan's fabricated character of Shayne Casper is Edan's best friend on Celco. Shayne both advises and comforts Edan in times of personal pain or doubt. His other friend—and girlfriend— is Dizzie, and it appears that Edan has developed sexual feelings and release by fantasising about a romantic relationship with Dizzie, now utilising his tights as an aide rather than as the primary focus towards achievement of an orgasm. The supreme ruler of Celco is Maxximossos the Fox, and Edan sleeps, eats, and enjoys recreational time with larger-than-life fox soft toys, even taking them on the rare walks he has in the local park with his carers.

The very real struggle felt by Edan to reach Celco at some point defines his perennial sacrifice to continue living on Earth, with his disability and mental anguish, but as discussed with Edan's behaviour therapist and GP, it is also a most necessary crutch for his day-to-day survival.

There are myriad quirks that can set off Edan's OCD attacks, such as our dogs or our cat shaking their heads (as if drying themselves off) and God only knows what more will come in the future.

On the 4th April 2023, Edan attended court for property damage, having been charged by the South Australian Police. He was dismissed with a fine. Shortly after this, the NDIA granted Edan a plan review funding of $1.555 million, which includes special disability housing, something only six per cent of NDIS clients receive in the state of South Australia.

I'll sign off now by saying that Asperger's syndrome/ASD is a family condition. We are all in it together, and if someone like Edan suffers, and he must, we are *all* dragged into his suffering. But, it's not all gloom and doom. Edan has an excellent sense of static humour. He views things so differently to us neurotypicals, adding a different and very raw dimension to situations and people, which is sometimes liberating and refreshing. Complete honesty and disclosure are most definitely attributes that mark the Aspie's personality, and in today's dog-eat-dog, treacherous, media-dominated society, a grain of technicolour, unadulterated truth is not such a bad thing.

I love you Edan,

Mum.

Inside an Aspie's imagination before the 'darker side'.

EDAN'S MENTALLY ILL STORY

I have autism and Asperger's syndrome, my mind is not normal, but in my twisted idea, it is normal to me.

I believe I don't belong in this world that you call Planet Earth. I have this really big problem where I absolutely despise with a huge strong passion about living in the universe I currently am, and that I wished I lived in a world that I really want to create called Celco!

I have feelings that I want to kill thousands and millions of people to the point where I'm even way worse than Adolf Hitler and then kill myselfonly because when I say I hate earth, it all comes down to people that I find cruel and ignorant! People are my target of hatred, rage, even jealousy. Reason is, is because I had history of encountering people on YouTube talkingabout really harsh things about other people only because they made some epic mistakes in the past and I always have to feel like I want to feel sorry for those people because of what the harsh people were saying about them. And then outside of watching YouTube, in the actual surroundings, I got mad at people and threatened to hurt them, shouted at them and saying the worst ugly swear words ever imagined to them because I felt there was ways why they made me so full of rage. It's because they say something that might have my feelings hurt or they talk about things that makes me feel like I don't have quite enough of the same luxury benefits as them.

Like for example I really really love the animal foxes, if I go to like a shopping centre and I see fox pictures on any printing device, my heart starts shaking with nerve because I get very jealous about the fact that I might feel foxes are so popular that it's even too good for me to handle, and I can't handle it all because I feel like I want to have the deepest strongest affection for foxes more than anyone in the entire world. And that's true because I happen to be an amazing artist. All my motivation techniques comes down to drawing, because drawing makes up this Celco world of mine and Celco is just like earth, but it's fa far more vast better fairy tale like version.

I draw pictures that represents Celco like the kind of inhabitants, animals and places and stuff and the reason why I get so angry is because I feel like the earth energy is preventing me from gaining access to Celco! Like the negative power from earth is corrupting my mind into thinking that things I do and how I run things in my special universe will never be as it seems. In a way that it is not Celco at all, it's actually Earth I'm seeing being very smug and getting in my face and laughing at my face!

What I say about me loving foxes is because I created a brand new fox pet called Maxximoss and he's like this super special fox that's like my guardian god that protects me from any harm. Now what I'm about to say is very shocking but me and Maxximoss think that murdering people is a good thing. Think about it, when the big bang theory started everything came into existence, then it came into people's thoughts, actions, voice of speech into what came from the rights or wrongs from god, or if god never existed, those acts of people will came from the birth place of nothing's orbital area.

Just so you know I believe there is two big bang theories and two heavens completely impassably divided from each other. One on the left, one on the right. The left side is just called the big bang, but the right side is called the big bang Armedorous. The left big bang is the version where there is more to life about strategies of how there is more of a chance of the existence that there is more of what you call the coping existence. Now this is where it gets very interesting, the right side, the big bang Armedorous is what you call the simple paradise existence. Celco is on the Armedorous side and I believe I happened to be on the left side, the coping existence. Coping existence means you have to go to school, do very difficult courses and trying very hard to get smart at university which I had a nightmare at, at doing TAFE that I just ditched classes. Having to use money everywhere you go, dealing with idiots in the world and having to have prisons when you commit a crime!

Now what would it be like living in a world where you don't have to have all those coping skills with you there. What if even you killed someone or anyone in particular and they can't die, they're invincible and they'll take that as a pranking joke!! Hahaha you can't kill me! I'm invincible! Celco is in another outer space, now how can that be when outer space goes for infinity so it's impossible for there to be two of them. Well to me that's not the case, there is a spirited unseeable barrier wall that divides the two orbits depending on which orbit is more real to you and the other orbit doesn't exist to you depending on which orbital universe you're on. Celco is so different from earth's universe that Celco's way of how it does things on it's livable planet is the way that things come from bizarre meaning that earth's meaning will never ever understand, but that's okay because I hate earth so much that I don't want to be here and I want to be on Celco.

I really like things that are bizarre and don't make sense, because you can just make sense out of them. It's called interest and discovery. Also with Armedorous outer space having its own version of heaven, that means that that version of god is a whole complete different god with different acts, and he makes things more simple for you.

Wait a second, I said it all wrong, there is no heaven on Armadorous because Celco is heaven itself because you're immortal plus you also have an eternal lifespan and god is already a being on Celco so it would be silly having heaven anyway. I somehow wish Armedorous could pick me up and carry me to itself somehow in a mystery phantom in the middle of my dream while I'm sleeping and then I could just vanish in thin air then I won't exist in this universe of despair anymore and exist on the right side instead. I even wished in order to do this, I could die of old happy age here on earth and go to the earth's heaven but then transfer my existing data to be reincarnated on Celco's universe and I want to have a special magical fox that kills people, but he does it in the kind and friendly way because you know what, nobody can die on Celco, so it would be used as a joke and you won't need police because of that. And it would make life so much more simple and clean, easy and fun. No school, no college, no money, everything in the world is free, and no stupid bullies whether on the internet or without.

Also I have this new happy family that supports me on Celco now too because I draw them as well. Their names are James, Angelica, Shayne and Dizzie. James and Angelica are the parents and Shayne and Dizzie are my little brother and sister. Dizzie is also my girlfriend at the same timeso that's the story and that's why I feel so angry and sad all the time and say I want to kill people or kill myself because I feel like it's the people to blame why I can't go on Celco, so please I really need your help ASAP and I need you to put me in a mental health facility to fix my brain up so that at least, while I'm still lasting on earth I can never ever feel so so so angry ever again and always think positive for the rest of my life and at least until I die of old age! I really want to be happy, cheerful, merriful!! So please I beg you help fix my brain and see what's going wrong with it, in a mental health facility because my mum requested the same thing to you guys too but no one is listening to her so can you guys please, please I beg you with all my heart listen to me, thank you for hearing my story, and I hope that all what I just told you really made a lot of sense to you.

(Top Left) Edan as the face of innocence.
(Bottom Left) Edan and his beloved foxes, 'Rulers of Celco'.
(Right) Bleeding and desperate, Edan self-harming following a four-hour showdown with Adam. Once the police and ambulance arrived, Edan was handcuffed and secured to the ambulance gurney due to his aggressive behaviour.

ACKNOWLEDGEMENTS

Dr. Scott Zarcinas, DoctorZed Publishing
Hari Teah, Editor
Dr. Tony Atwood, Clinical Psychologist and world authority on Asperger's Syndrome and ASD
Kirsty Moore, Clinical Psychologist
Sophie Rowe, Behaviour Support Practitioner
Lily Nicholls, Occupational Therapist
Natalie Mudge, NDIS Support Co-ordinator
Walter Kokadovic, House Manager, Always Care Disability Services
Dipleen Arneja, CEO AEON Disability Services
Jim Bowden and Leeanne Halfpenny, Edan's former employers
The Rachwal Family
Adam Brewer, Edan's Stepfather
Kristen Galbraith, Edan's Sister
Alycia Galbraith, Edan's Sister
Lee Casuscelli
Robbie Rogers
Niko Gambeli
Sabrina Schwalger
'Pat'

www.ingramcontent.com/pod-product-compliance
Lightning Source LLC
LaVergne TN
LVHW051554070426
835507LV00021B/2579